EDITED BY JANE
ILLUSTR/

C000001827

FAVOURITE
POEMS

Over 120 classic poems
to inspire, comfort and delight

Editor's dedication: To Mat and Tabitha

Illustrator's dedication: To Clive, Rosie and Hannah

First published in the United Kingdom in 2017 by
National Trust Books
43 Great Ormond Street
London WC1N 3HZ

An imprint of Pavilion Books Company Ltd

Edition © National Trust Books, 2017
Illustrations © Jane Robbins, 2017

The National Trust is a registered charity, No. 205846

All rights reserved. No part of this publication may be reproduced,
stored in a retrieval system, or transmitted in any form or by any means,
mechanical, photocopying, recording or otherwise, without the prior
permission of the copyright owner.

ISBN: 9781911358213

A CIP catalogue record for this book is available from
the British Library.

22 21 20 19 18
10 9 8 7 6 5 4 3 2

Reproduction by ColourDepth, UK
Printed by Toppan Leefung Printing Ltd, China

This book can be ordered direct from the publisher at the website
www.pavilionbooks.com, or try your local bookshop. Also available at
National Trust shops, including www.nationaltrustbooks.co.uk

Contents

Beasts and Birds: 'Velvet Footsteps'

The Sea: 'Along the Sand'

Journeys: 'I Travelled among Unknown Men'

War: 'The Noise of Battle'

Old Favourites: 'Green and Pleasant Land'

Introduction

Most people have a favourite poem, even if it is only a half-remembered fragment from school. Many popular poems are also remembered for personal reasons: a piece read at a wedding or funeral, or one that brings back particular memories. However the majority of poets do not like to be remembered for a single piece. Yeats grew to hate 'The Lake Isle of Innisfree' as he felt his entire life's work could not be summed up in a mere twelve lines and, despite his vast output, Wordsworth is most often remembered for describing a hillside of daffodils. Without an infinite amount of time (and space in an anthology) though, we all have to be selective. It is better to be remembered for one poem than entirely forgotten and I hope this collection will remind the reader of poets as well as poems.

Many National Trust properties are mentioned in poetry and, over the years, some owners have even been poets. The 1st Earl of Dorset, whose houses included Knole, Kent, wrote verse, sadly no longer well-known enough to include here, while later the 6th Earl was an important patron to a number of poets including Alexander Pope, John Dryden and Matthew Prior; Pope wrote his flattering epitaph, 'Dorset, the grace of courts, the Muses' pride'. Less flatteringly he described the 2nd Lord Hervey of Ickworth, Suffolk, as 'that mere white Curd of Ass's Milk'. John Dryden's family owned Canons Ashby, Northamptonshire, and he and Edmund Spenser were both frequent visitors to the house, while Milton, Shakespeare and Pope are commemorated at the Temple of British Worthies at Stowe, Buckinghamshire. After the poems with a particular National Trust connection there is a brief description of the place or property. Tennyson's 'June Bracken and Heather' is a beautiful poem but much more so if one reads it standing on the Isle of Wight where Tennyson would have stood with his wife. Equally *The Garden* by Vita Sackville-West should really be read sitting on a bench in the garden at Sissinghurst, Kent, where the poem was written.

Where practicable I have included the entire poem in a version as close to the original as possible. Even so, some poems had to be cut. The first nine verses of Gray's 'Elegy Written in a Country Churchyard' stand well on their own and the opening stanzas of Poe's 'The Raven' and Wilde's *The Ballad of Reading Gaol* introduce us to the story and will, I hope, entice the reader to seek out the entire poem. Others, such as Tennyson's 'The Palace of Art', which includes the wonderful description of the National Trust's Gunby Hall in Lincolnshire as 'a haunt of ancient peace', do not cut so well and, sadly, had to be omitted.

The poems are divided into sections but many cross the boundaries; sticking strictly to subject matter would have resulted in an unwieldy section on love and an almost as unwieldy one on death. Instead I have followed Laurence Durrell's strategy, 'I have always tried to arrange my poems for balanced readability – like one does a vase of flowers'. Included in this vase are, I hope, the majority of poems most readers would expect to find, plus a few pleasant surprises that will become future favourites.

Life

'Gather Ye

Rose-buds While Ye May'

Monday's Child

Monday's child is fair of face,
Tuesday's child is full of grace,
Wednesday's child is full of woe,
Thursday's child has far to go,
Friday's child is loving and giving,
Saturday's child works hard for his living,
And the child that is born on the Sabbath day
Is bonny and blithe, and good and gay.

Anon

The Little Dancers

Lonely, save for a few faint stars, the sky
Dreams; and lonely, below, the little street
Into its gloom retires, secluded and shy.
Scarcely the dumb roar enters this soft retreat;
And all is dark, save where come flooding rays
From a tavern-window; there, to the brisk measure
Of an organ that down in the alley merrily plays,
Two children, all alone and no one by,
Holding their tattered frocks, thro' an airy maze
Of motion lightly threaded with nimble feet
Dance sedately; face to face they gaze,
Their eyes shining, grave with a perfect pleasure.

Laurence Binyon
(1869–1943)

Piano

Softly, in the dusk, a woman singing to me;
Taking me back down the vista of years, till I see
A child sitting under the piano, in the boom of the tingling strings
And pressing the small, poised feet of the mother who smiles as she sings.

In spite of myself, the insidious mastery of song
Betrays me back, till the heart of me weeps to belong
To the old Sunday evenings at home, with winter outside
And hymns in the cosy parlour, the tinkling piano our guide.

So now it is in vain for the singer to burst into clamour
With the great black piano appassionato. The glamour
Of childish days is upon me, my manhood is cast
Down in the flood of remembrance, I weep like a child for the past.

D. H. Lawrence
(1885–1930)

Boys and Girls

What are little boys made of?
       Frogs and snails
       And puppy-dogs' tails,
That's what little boys are made of.

What are little girls made of?
       Sugar and spice
       And all things nice,
That's what little girls are made of.

Anon

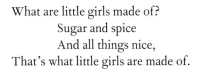

The Schoolboy

from: *Songs of Experience*

I love to rise in a summer morn,
When the birds sing on every tree;
The distant huntsman winds his horn,
And the skylark sings with me:
O what sweet company!

But to go to school in a summer morn, -
O it drives all joy away!
Under a cruel eye outworn,
The little ones spend the day
In sighing and dismay.

Ah then at times I drooping sit,
And spend many an anxious hour;
Nor in my book can I take delight,
Nor sit in learning's bower,
Worn through with the dreary shower.

How can the bird that is born for joy
Sit in a cage and sing?
How can a child, when fears annoy,
But droop his tender wing,
And forget his youthful spring!

O father and mother if buds are nipped,
And blossoms blown away;
And if the tender plants are stripped
Of their joy in the springing day,
By sorrow and care's dismay, -

How shall the summer arise in joy,
Or the summer fruits appear?
Or how shall we gather what griefs destroy,
Or bless the mellowing year,
When the blasts of winter appear?

William Blake
(1757–1827)

Skating in the Evening
from: *The Prelude*

And in the frosty season, when the sun
Was set, and visible for many a mile
The cottage windows blazed through the twilight gloom,
I heeded not their summons: happy time
It was indeed for all of us – for me
It was a time of rapture! Clear and loud
The village clock tolled six, – I wheeled about,
Proud and exalting like an untired horse
That cares not for his home. All shod with steel.
We hissed along the polished ice in games
Confederate, imitative of the chase
And woodland pleasures, – the resounding horn,
The pack loud chiming, and the hunted hare.

So through the darkness and the cold we flew,
And not a voice was idle; with the din
Smitten, the precipices rang aloud;
The leafless trees and every icy crag
Tinkled like iron; while far distant hills
Into the tumult sent an alien sound
Of melancholy not unnoticed, while the stars
Eastward were sparkling clear, and in the west
The orange sky of evening died away.
Not seldom from the uproar I retired
Into a silent bay, or sportively
Glanced sideway, leaving the tumultuous throng,
To cut across the reflex of a star
That fled, and, flying still before me, gleamed
Upon the glassy plain; and oftentimes,
When we had given our bodies to the wind,
And all the shadowy banks on either side
Came sweeping through the darkness, spinning still
The rapid line of motion, then at once
Have I, reclining back upon my heels,
Stopped short; yet still the solitary cliffs
Wheeled by me – even as if the earth had rolled
With visible motion her diurnal round!
Behind me they did stretch in solemn train,
Feebler and feebler, and I stood and watched
Till all was tranquil as in a dreamless sleep.

William Wordsworth
(1770–1850)

Wordsworth began his autobiographical poem *The Prelude* in his twenties and worked on
it throughout his life. It recalls his happy childhood at the family home in Cockermouth,
Cumbria, now owned by the National Trust and called Wordsworth House.

Fern Hill

Now as I was young and easy under the apple boughs
About the lilting house and happy as the grass was green,
  The night above the dingle starry,
    Time let me hail and climb
  Golden in the heydays of his eyes,
And honoured among wagons I was prince of the apple towns
And once below a time I lordly had the trees and leaves
    Trail with daisies and barley
  Down the rivers of the windfall light.

And as I was green and carefree, famous among the barns
About the happy yard and singing as the farm was home,
  In the sun that is young once only,
    Time let me play and be
  Golden in the mercy of his means,
And green and golden I was huntsman and herdsman, the calves
Sand to my horn, the foxes on the hills barked clear and cold,
    And the sabbath rang slowly
  In the pebbles of the holy streams.

All the sun long it was running, it was lovely, the hay
Fields high as the house, the tunes from the chimneys, it was air
  And playing, lovely and watery
    And fire green as grass.
  And nightly under the simple stars
As I rode to sleep the owls were bearing the farm away,
All the moon long I heard, blessed among the stables, the nightjars
    Flying with the ricks, and the horses
    Flashing into the dark.

And then to awake, and the farm, like a wanderer white
With the dew, come back, the cock on his shoulder: it was all
      Shining, it was Adam and maiden,
          The sky gathered again
      And the sun grew round that very day.
So it must have been after the birth of the simple light
In the first, spinning place, the spellbound horses walking warm
      Out of the whinnying green stable
          On to the fields of praise.

And honoured among foxes and pheasants by the gay house
Under the new made clouds and happy as the heart was long,
      In the sun born over and over,
          I ran my heedless ways,
      My wishes raced through the house high hay
And nothing I cared, at my sky blue trades, that time allows
In all his tuneful turning so few and such morning songs
      Before the children green and golden
          Follow him out of grace,

Nothing I cared, in the lamb white days, that time would take me
Up to the swallow thronged loft by the shadow of my hand,
      In the moon that is always rising,
          Nor that riding to sleep
      I should hear him fly with the high fields
And wake to the farm forever fled from the childless land.
Oh as I was young and easy in the mercy of his means,
      Time held me green and dying
      Though I sang in my chains like the sea.

Dylan Thomas
(1914–1953)

To the Virgins, to make much of Time

Gather ye Rose-buds while ye may,
     Old Time is still a flying:
And this same flower that smiles to day,
     To morrow will be dying.

The glorious Lamp of Heaven, the Sun,
     The higher he's a getting;
The sooner will his Race be run,
     And neerer he's to Setting.

That Age is best, which is the first,
     When Youth and Blood are warmer;
But being spent, the worst, and worst
     Times, still succeed the former.

Then be not coy, but use your time;
     And while ye may, goe marry:
For having lost but once your prime,
     You may for ever tarry.

Robert Herrick
(1591–1674)

To My Dear and Loving Husband

If ever two were one, then surely we.
If ever man were loved by wife, then thee;
If ever wife was happy in a man,
Compare with me, ye women, if you can.
I prize thy love more than whole mines of gold
Or all the riches that the East doth hold.
My love is such that rivers cannot quench,
Nor ought but love from thee, give recompense.
Thy love is such I can no way repay,
The heavens reward thee manifold, I pray.
Then while we live, in love let's so persevere
That when we live no more, we may live for ever.

Anne Bradstreet
(c.1612–1672)

Love and Age

I played with you 'mid cowslips blowing,
When I was six and you were four;
When garlands weaving, flower-balls throwing,
Were pleasures soon to please no more.
Through groves and meads, o'er grass and heather,
With little playmates, to and fro,
We wandered hand in hand together;
But that was sixty years ago.

You grew a lovely roseate maiden,
And still our early love was strong;
Still with no care our days were laden,
They glided joyously along;
And I did love you, very dearly,
How dearly words want power to show;
I thought your heart was touched as nearly;
But that was fifty years ago.

Then other lovers came around you,
Your beauty grew from year to year,
And many a splendid circle found you
The centre of its glistening sphere.
I saw you then, first vows forsaking,
On rank and wealth your hand bestow;
Oh, then I thought my heart was breaking, –
But that was forty years ago.

And I lived on, to wed another:
No cause she gave me to repine;
And when I heard you were a mother,
I did not wish the children mine.
My own young flock, in fair progression,
Made up a pleasant Christmas row:
My joy in them was past expression; –
But that was thirty years ago.

You grew a matron plump and comely,
You dwelt in fashion's brightest blaze;
My earthly lot was far more homely;
But I too had my festal days.
No merrier eyes have ever glistened
Around the hearth-stone's wintry glow,
Than when my youngest child was christened: –
But that was twenty years ago.

Time passed. My eldest girl was married,
And now I am a grandsire grey;
One pet of four years old I've carried
Among the wild-flowered meads to play.
In our old fields of childish pleasure,
Where now as then, the cowslips blow,
She fills her basket's ample measure, –
And that is not ten years ago.

But though love's first impassioned blindness
Has passed away in colder light,
I still have thought of you with kindness,
And shall do, till our last good-night.
The ever-rolling silent hours
Will bring a time we shall not know,
When our young days of gathering flowers
Will be a hundred years ago.

Thomas Love Peacock
(1785–1866)

So, we'll go no more a roving

I

So, we'll go no more a roving
    So late into the night,
Though the heart be still as loving,
    And the moon be still as bright.

II

For the sword outwears its sheath,
    And the soul outwears the breast,
And the heart must pause to breathe,
    And love itself have rest.

III

Though the night was made for loving,
    And the day returns too soon,
Yet we'll go no more a roving
    By the light of the moon.

George Gordon, Lord Byron
(1788–1824)

When You Are Old

When you are old and grey and full of sleep,
And nodding by the fire, take down this book,
And slowly read, and dream of the soft look
Your eyes had once, and of their shadows deep;

How many loved your moments of glad grace,
And loved your beauty with love false or true,
But one man loved the pilgrim soul in you,
And loved the sorrows of your changing face;

And bending down beside the glowing bars,
Murmur, a little sadly, how Love fled
And paced upon the mountains overhead
And hid his face amid a crowd of stars.

W. B. Yeats
(1865–1939)

Love
'The Life
That I
Have
is
Yours'

The Passionate Shepherd to his Love

Come live with me and be my love,
And we will all the pleasures prove,
That hills and valleys, dales and fields,
And all the craggy mountains yields.

There we will sit upon the rocks,
And see the shepherds feed their flocks,
By shallow rivers to whose falls
Melodious birds sing madrigals.

And I will make thee beds of roses
With a thousand fragrant posies,
A cap of flowers, and a kirtle,
Embroidered all with leaves of myrtle;

A gown made of the finest wool
Which from our pretty lambs we pull;
Fair lined slippers for the cold,
With buckles of the purest gold;

A belt of straw and ivy-buds,
With coral clasps and amber studs:
And if these pleasures may thee move,
Come live with me and be my love.

The shepherds' swains shall dance and sing
For thy delight each May morning:
If these delights thy mind may move,
Then live with me and be my love.

Christopher Marlowe
(c. 1564–1593)

First Love

I ne'er was struck before that hour
      With love so sudden and so sweet.
Her face it bloomed like a sweet flower
      And stole my heart away complete.
My face turned pale as deadly pale.
      My legs refused to walk away,
And when she looked, 'what could I ail?'
      My life and all seemed turned to clay.

And then my blood rushed to my face
      And took my eyesight quite away.
The trees and bushes round the place
      Seemed midnight at noonday.
I could not see a single thing,
      Words from my eyes did start;
They spoke as chords do from the string
      And blood burnt round my heart.

Are flowers the winter's choice?
      Is love's bed always snow?
She seemed to hear my silent voice
      Not love's appeals to know.
I never saw so sweet a face
      As that I stood before:
My heart has left its dwelling place
      And can return no more.

John Clare
(1793–1864)

To his Coy Mistress

Had we but World enough, and Time,
This coyness Lady were no crime.
We would sit down and think which way
To walk, and pass our long Loves Day.
Thou by the *Indian Ganges* side
Should'st Rubies find: I by the Tide
Of *Humber* would complain, I would
Love you ten years before the Flood:
And you should if you please refuse
Till the Conversion of the Jews.
My vegetable Love should grow
Vaster than Empires, and more slow.
An hundred years should go to praise
Thine Eyes, and on thy Forehead Gaze.
Two hundred to adore each Breast:
But thirty thousand to the rest.
An Age at least to every part,
And the last Age should show your Heart.
For Lady you deserve this State;
Nor would I love at lower rate.
      But at my back I alwaies hear
Times wingèd Charriot hurrying near:
And yonder all before us lye
Desarts of vast Eternity.
Thy Beauty shall no more be found;
Nor, in thy marble Vault, shall sound
My ecchoing Song: then Worms shall try
That long preserv'd Virginity:
And your quaint Honour turn to dust;
And into ashes all my Lust.
The Grave's a fine and private place,
But none I think do there embrace.

Now therefore, while the youthful hew
Sits on thy skin like morning dew,
And while thy willing Soul transpires
At every pore with instant Fires,
Now let us sport us while we may;
And now, like am'rous birds of prey,
Rather at once our Time devour,
Than languish in his slow-chapt pow'r.
Let us roll all our Strength, and all
Our sweetness, up into one Ball;
And tear our Pleasures with rough strife,
Thorough the Iron gates of Life.
Thus, though we cannot make our Sun
Stand still, yet we will make him run.

Andrew Marvell
(1621–1678)

Sonnet XXX

Love is not all: it is not meat or drink
Nor slumber nor a roof against the rain;
Nor yet a floating spar to men that sink
And rise and sink and rise and sink again;
Love cannot fill the thickened lung with breath,
Nor clean the blood, nor set the fractured bone;
Yet many a man is making friends with death
Even as I speak, for lack of love alone.
It may well be that in a difficult hour,
Pinned down by pain and moaning for release,
Or nagged by want past resolution's power,
I might be driven to sell your love for peace,
Or trade the memory of this night for food.
It may well be. I do not think I would.

Edna St Vincent Millay
(1892–1950)

Love Without Hope

Love without hope, as when the young bird-catcher
Swept off his tall hat to the Squire's own daughter,
So let the imprisoned larks escape and fly
Singing about her head, as she rode by.

Robert Graves
(1895–1985)

Charita

from: *The Countess of Pembroke's Arcadia*

My true love hath my hart, and I have his,
By just exchange, one for the other giv'ne.
I holde his deare, and myne he cannot misse:
There never was a better bargain driv'ne.

His hart in me, keepes me and him in one,
My hart in him, his thoughtes and senses guides:
He loves my hart, for once it was his owne:
I cherish his, because in me it bides.

His hart his wound receaved from my sight:
My hart was wounded, with his wounded hart,
For as from me, on him his hurt did light,
So still me thought in me his hurt did smart:
      Both equall hurt, in this change sought our blisse:
      My true love hath my hart and I have his.

Sir Philip Sidney
(1554–1586)

Sonnet XVIII

Shall I compare thee to a Summers day?
Thou art more lovely and more temperate:
Rough windes do shake the darling buds of Maie,
And Sommers lease hath all to short a date:
Sometime too hot the eye of heaven shines,
And often is his gold complexion dimm'd,
And every faire from faire some-time declines,
By chance, or natures changing course untrim'd:
But thy eternall Sommer shall not fade,
Nor lose possession of that faire thou ow'st,
Nor shall death brag thou wandr'st in his shade,
When in eternall lines to time thou grow'st,
      So long as men can breathe or eyes can see,
      So long lives this, and gives life to thee.

William Shakespeare
(1564–1616)

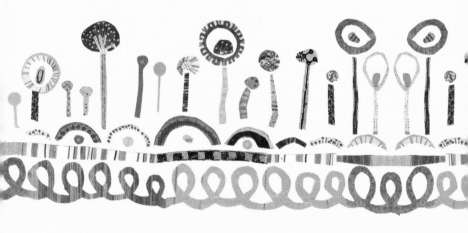

Sonnet XLIII
from: *Sonnets from the Portuguese*

How do I love thee? Let me count the ways.
I love thee to the depth and breadth and height
My soul can reach, when feeling out of sight
For the ends of Being and ideal Grace.
I love thee to the level of every day's
Most quiet need, by sun and candle light.
I love thee freely, as men strive for Right;
I love thee purely, as they turn from Praise.
I love thee with the passion put to use
In my old griefs, and with my childhood's faith.
I love thee with a love I seemed to lose
With my lost saints, – I love thee with the breath,
Smiles, tears, of all my life! – and, if God chose,
I shall but love thee better after death.

Elizabeth Barrett Browning
(1806–1861)

The Life That I Have

The life that I have
Is all that I have
And the life that I have
Is yours.

The love that I have
Of the life that I have
Is yours and yours and yours.

A sleep I shall have
A rest I shall have
Yet death will be but a pause.

For the peace of my years
In the long green grass
Will be yours and yours and yours.

Leo Marks
(1920–2001)

Written on Christmas Eve 1943 for Ruth, a girl with whom Leo Marks was in love, who had been killed in a plane crash in Canada. The following year he gave it to the agent Violette Szabo to use as the cipher for encoding her messages from France.

Sonnet CXVI

Let me not to the marriage of true minds
Admit impediments. Love is not love
Which alters when it alteration finds,
Or bends with the remover to remove.
O no, it is an ever-fixèd mark
That looks on tempests and is never shaken;
It is the star to every wand'ring barque,
Whose worth's unknown, although his height be taken.
Love's not time's fool, though rosy lips and cheeks
Within his bending sickle's compass come;
Love alters not with his brief hours and weeks,
But bears it out even to the edge of doom.
      If this be error and upon me proved,
      I never writ, nor no man ever loved.

William Shakespeare
(1564–1616)

Sonnet

Bright star, would I were stedfast as thou art —
    Not in lone splendour hung aloft the night
And watching, with eternal lids apart,
    Like nature's patient, sleepless Eremite,
The moving waters at their priestlike task
    Of pure ablution round earth's human shores,
Or grazing on the new soft-fallen mask
    Of snow upon the mountains and the moors —
No — yet still stedfast, still unchangeable,
    Pillow'd upon my fair love's ripening breast,
To feel for ever its soft fall and swell,
    Awake for ever in a sweet unrest,
Still, still to hear her tender-taken breath,
And so live ever — or else swoon to death.

John Keats
(1795–1821)

June Bracken and Heather
TO –

There on the top of the down,
The wild heather round me and over me June's high blue,
When I look'd down at the bracken so bright and the heather
          so brown,
I thought to myself I would offer this book to you,
This, and my love together,
To you that are seventy-seven,
With a faith as clear as the heights of the June-blue heaven,
And a fancy as summer-new
As the green of the bracken amid the gloom of the heather.

Alfred, Lord Tennyson
(1809–1892)

In 1853 Tennyson moved to the Isle of Wight. Much of his poetry was composed on the
long walks he took every day, especially along High Down (now called Tennyson Down),
the imposing cliffs that stretch from Freshwater Bay to the Needles. This poem was
written in 1891 to his wife Emily for their forty-first wedding anniversary.

An Arundel Tomb

Side by side, their faces blurred,
The earl and countess lie in stone,
Their proper habits vaguely shown
As jointed armour, stiffened pleat,
And that faint hint of the absurd –
The little dog under their feet.

Such plainness of the pre-baroque
Hardly involves the eye, until
It meets his left-hand gauntlet, still
Clasped empty in the other; and
One sees, with a sharp tender shock,
His hand withdrawn, holding her hand.

They would not think to lie so long.
Such faithfulness in effigy
Was just a detail friends would see:
A sculptor's sweet commissioned grace
Thrown off in helping to prolong
The Latin names around the base.

They would not guess how early in
Their supine stationary voyage
The air would change to soundless damage,
Turn the tenantry away;
How soon succeeding eyes begin
To look, not read. Rigidly they

Persisted, linked, through lengths and breadths
Of time. Snow fell, undated. Light
Each summer thronged the glass. A bright
Litter of birdcalls strewed the same
Bone-riddled ground. And up the paths
The endless altered people came,

Washing at their identity.
Now, helpless in the hollow of
An unarmorial age, a trough
Of smoke in slow suspended skeins
Above their scrap of history,
Only an attitude remains:

Time has transfigured them into
Untruth. The stone fidelity
They hardly meant has come to be
Their final blazon, and to prove
Our almost-instinct almost true:
What will survive of us is love.

Philip Larkin
(1922–1985)

Loss
'With
a Wistful
Eye'

Because I Could Not Stop

Because I could not stop for Death –
He kindly stopped for me –
The Carriage held but just Ourselves –
And Immortality.

We slowly drove – He knew no haste
And I had put away
My labor and my leisure too,
For His Civility –

We passed the School, where Children strove
At Recess – in the Ring –
We passed the Fields of Gazing Grain –
We passed the Setting Sun –

Or rather – He passed Us –
The Dews drew quivering and chill –
For only Gossamer, my Gown –
My Tippet - only Tulle –

We paused before a House that seemed
A Swelling of the Ground –
The Roof was scarcely visible –
The Cornice – in the Ground –

Since then – 'tis Centuries – and yet
Feels shorter than the Day
I first surmised the Horses' Heads
Were toward Eternity –

Emily Dickinson
(1830–1886)

The Ballad of Reading Gaol

In Memoriam
C. T. W.
Sometime Trooper of the Royal Horse Guards.
Obiit HM Prison, Reading, Berkshire,
July 7th, 1896.

Verses 1–9

He did not wear his scarlet coat,
    For blood and wine are red,
And blood and wine were on his hands
    When they found him with the dead,
The poor dead woman whom he loved,
    And murdered in her bed.

He walked amongst the Trial men
    In a suit of shabby gray;
A cricket cap was on his head,
    And his step seemed light and gay;
But I never saw a man who looked
    So wistfully at the day.

I never saw a man who looked
    With such a wistful eye
Upon that little tent of blue
    Which prisoners call the sky,
And at every drifting cloud that went
    With sails of silver by.

I walked, with other souls in pain,
    Within another ring,
And was wondering if the man had done
    A great or little thing,
When a voice behind me whispered low,
    'That fellow's got to swing.'

Dear Christ! the very prison walls
      Suddenly seemed to reel,
And the sky above my head became
      Like a casque of scorching steel;
And, though I was a soul in pain,
      My pain I could not feel.

I only knew what hunted thought
      Quickened his steps, and why
He looked upon the garish day
      With such a wistful eye;
The man had killed the thing he loved,
      And so he had to die.
            *

Yet each man kills the thing he loves,
      By each let this be heard,
Some do it with a bitter look,
      Some with a flattering word,
The coward does it with a kiss,
      The brave man with a sword!

Some kill their love when they are young,
      And some when they are old;
Some strangle with the hands of Lust,
      Some with the hands of Gold:
The kindest use a knife, because
      The dead so soon grow cold.

Some love too little, some too long,
      Some sell, and others buy;
Some do the deeds with many tears,
      And some without a sigh:
For each man kills the thing he loves,
      Yet each man does not die.

Oscar Wilde
(1854–1900)

XXVII

from: *In Memoriam A. H. H.*

I envy not in any moods
      The captive void of noble rage,
      The linnet born within the cage,
That never knew the summer woods:

I envy not the beast that takes
      His license in the field of time,
      Unfettered by the sense of crime,
To whom a conscience never wakes;

Nor, what may count itself as blest,
      The heart that never plighted troth
      But stagnates in the weeds of sloth;
Nor any want-begotten rest.

I hold it true, what e'er befall;
      I feel it when I sorrow most;
      'Tis better to have loved and lost
Than never to have loved at all.

Alfred, Lord Tennyson
(1809–1892)

Sir William Dyer

Monument to Sir William Dyer, erected by his wife in 1641,
St Denys Church, Colmworth

If a large hart, joynd with a noble mind
Shewing true worth, unto all good inclind
If faith in friendship, justice unto all,
Leave such a memory as we may call
Happy, thine is; then pious marble keepe
His just fame waking, though his lov'd dust sleepe.
And though death can devoure all that hath breath,
And monuments them selves have had a death,
Nature shan't suffer this, to ruinate,
Nor time demolish't, nor an envious fate,
Rais'd by just a hand, not vaine glorious pride,
Who'd be conceal'd, wer't modesty to hide
Such an affection did so long survive
The object of 't; yet lov'd it as alive.
And this greate blessing to his name doth give
To make it by his tombe, and issue live.

My dearest dust could not thy hasty day
Afford thy drowzy patience leave to stay
One hower longer: so that wee might either
Sate up, or gone to bedd together?
But since thy finisht labor hath possessed
Thy weary limbs with early rest,
Enjoy it sweetly; and thy widdowe bride
Shall soone repose her by thy slumbring side;
Whose business, now, is only to prepare
My nightly dress, and call to prayer:
Mine eyes wax heavy and the day grows old.
The dew falls thick, my bloud grows cold.
Draw, draw the closed curtaynes: and make room:
My deare, my dearest dust; I come, I come.

Katherine, Lady Dyer
(d.1654)

Song

When I am dead, my dearest,
     Sing no sad songs for me;
Plant thou no roses at my head,
     Nor shady cypress tree:
Be the green grass above me
     With showers and dewdrops wet:
And if thou wilt, remember,
     And if thou wilt, forget.

I shall not see the shadows,
     I shall not feel the rain;
I shall not hear the nightingale
     Sing on as if in pain:
And dreaming through the twilight
     That doth not rise nor set,
Haply I may remember,
     And haply may forget.

Christina Rossetti
(1830–1894)

Do not go gentle into that good night

Do not go gentle into that good night,
Old age should burn and rage at close of day;
Rage, rage against the dying of the light.

Though wise men at their end know dark is right,
Because their words had forked no lightning they
Do not go gentle into that good night.

Good men, the last wave by, crying how bright
Their frail deeds might have danced in a green bay,
Rage, rage against the dying of the light.

Wild men who caught and sang the sun in flight,
And learn, too late, they grieved it on its way,
Do not go gentle into that good night.

Grave men, near death, who see with blinding sight
Blind eyes could blaze like meteors and be gay,
Rage, rage against the dying of the light.

And you, my father, there on the sad height,
Curse, bless, me now with your fierce tears, I pray.
Do not go gentle into that good night.
Rage, rage against the dying of the light.

Dylan Thomas
(1914–1953)

A Valediction forbidding mourning

As virtuous men passe mildly away,
      And whisper to their soules, to goe,
Whist some of their sad friends doe say,
      The breath goes now, and some say, no.

So let us melt, and make no noise,
      No teare-floods, nor sigh-tempests move,
T'were prophanation of our joyes
      To tell the layetie our love.

Moving of th'earth brings harmes and feares,
      Men reckon what it did and meant,
But trepidation of the spheares,
      Though greater farre, is innocent.

Dull sublunary lovers love
      (Whose soule is sense) cannot admit
Absence, because it doth remove
      Those things which elemented it.

But we by a love, so much refin'd,
      That our selves know not what it is,
Inter-assured of the mind,
      Care lesse, eyes, lips, hands to misse.

Our two soules therefore, which are one,
      Though I must goe, endure not yet
A breach, but an expansion,
      Like gold to ayery thinnesse beate.

If they be two, they are two so
      As stiffe twin compasses are two,
Thy soul the fixt foot, makes no show
      To move, but doth, if the'other doe.

And though it in the center sit,
     Yet when the other far doth rome,
It leanes, and hearkens after it,
     And growes erect, as that comes home.

Such wilt thou be to mee, who must
     Like th'other foot, obliquely runne.
Thy firmness makes my circle just,
     And makes me end, where I begunne.

John Donne
(1572–1631)

Stop the Clocks
from: *Twelve Songs*

Stop all the clocks, cut off the telephone,
Prevent the dog from barking with a juicy bone,
Silence the pianos and with muffled drum
Bring out the coffin, let the mourners come.

Let aeroplanes circle moaning overhead
Scribbling on the sky the message He Is Dead,
Put crêpe bows round the white necks of the public doves,
Let traffic policemen wear black cotton gloves.

He was my North, my South, my East, my West,
My working week and my Sunday rest,
My noon, my midnight, my talk, my song;
I thought that love would last for ever: I was wrong.

The stars are not wanted now: put out every one;
Pack up the moon and dismantle the sun;
Pour away the ocean and sweep up the wood;
For nothing now can ever come to any good.

W. H. Auden
(1907–1973)

Remember

Remember me when I am gone away,
  Gone far away into the silent land;
  When you can no more hold me by the hand,
Nor I half turn to go yet turning stay.
Remember me when no more day by day
  You tell me of our future that you planned:
  Only remember me; you understand
It will be late to counsel then or pray.
Yet if you should forget me for a while
  And afterwards remember, do not grieve:
  For if the darkness and corruption leave
  A vestige of the thoughts that once I had,
Better by far you should forget and smile
  Than that you should remember and be sad.

Christina Rossetti
(1830–1894)

Do Not Stand at my Grave and Weep

Do not stand at my grave and weep
I am not there.
I do not sleep.
I am a thousand winds that blow
I am the diamond glints on snow.
I am the sunlight on ripened grain
I am the gentle autumn rain.
When you awaken in the morning's hush,
I am the swift uplifting rush
Of quiet birds in circled flight.
I am the soft stars that shine at night.
Do not stand at my grave and cry,
I am not there;
I did not die.

Mary Elizabeth Frye
(1905–2004)

Crossing the Bar

Sunset and evening star,
    And one clear call for me!
And may there be no moaning of the bar,
    When I put out to sea,

But such a tide as moving seems asleep,
    Too full for sound and foam,
When that which drew from out the boundless deep
    Turns again home.

Twilight and evening bell,
    And after that the dark!
And may there be no sadness of farewell,
    When I embark;

For tho' from out our bourne of Time and Place
    The flood may bear me far,
I hope to see my Pilot face to face
    When I have crost the bar.

Alfred, Lord Tennyson
(1809–1892)

The Seasons

'Dancing

in the

Breeze'

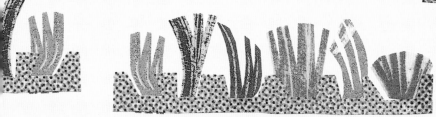

Weathers

I

This is the weather the cuckoo likes,
    And so do I;
When showers betumble the chestnut spikes,
    And nestlings fly:
And the little brown nightingale bills his best,
And they sit outside at 'The Travellers' Rest',
And maids come forth sprig-muslin drest,
And citizens dream of the south and west,
    And so do I.

II

This is the weather the shepherd shuns,
    And so do I;
When beeches drip in browns and duns,
    And thresh, and ply;
And hill-hid tides throb, throe on throe,
And meadow rivulets overflow,
And drops on gate-bars hang in a row,
And rooks in families homeward go,
    And so do I.

Thomas Hardy
(1840–1928)

Hardy lived in Dorset for most of his life, first at Higher Brockhampton (in what's now known as Hardy's Cottage) and later just three miles away at Max Gate. Many of the images in his writing come from the surrounding countryside. Hardy designed Max Gate himself and his third study has large windows without mullions and transoms at the centre so that he had clear view of the seasonal changes in the garden.

II

from: *A Shropshire Lad*

Loveliest of trees, the cherry now
Is hung with bloom along the bough,
And stands about the woodlands ride
Wearing white for Eastertide.

Now, of my threescore years and ten,
Twenty will not come again,
And take from seventy springs a score,
It only leaves me fifty more.

And since to look at things in bloom
Fifty springs are little room,
About the woodlands I will go
To see the cherry hung with snow.

A. E. Housman
(1859–1936)

The Lilac is in Bloom
from: *The Old Vicarage, Grantchester*
(*Café des Westens, Berlin, May 1912*)

Just now the lilac is in bloom,
All before my little room;
And in my flower-beds, I think,
Smile the carnations and the pink;
And down the borders, well I know,
The poppy and the pansy blow....
Oh! there the chestnuts, summer through,
Beside the river make for you
A tunnel of green gloom, and sleep
Deeply above; and green and deep
The stream mysterious glides beneath,
Green as a dream and deep as death.
 – Oh, damn! I know it! and I know
How the May fields all golden show,
And when the day is young and sweet,
Gild gloriously the bare feet
That run to bathe......

        Ah God! to see the branches stir
Across the moon at Grantchester!
To smell the thrilling-sweet and rotten
Unforgettable, unforgotten
River-smell, and hear the breeze
Sobbing in the little trees.
Say, do the elm-clumps greatly stand
Still guardians of that holy land?
The chestnuts shade, in reverend dream,
The yet unacademic stream?
Is dawn a secret shy and cold
Anadyomene, silver and gold?
And sunset still a golden sea
From Haslingfield to Madingley?

And after, ere the night is born,
Do hares come out about the corn?
Oh, is the water sweet and cool,
Gentle and brown, above the pool?
And laughs the immortal river still
Under the mill, under the mill?
Say, is there Beauty yet to find?
And Certainty? and Quiet kind?
Deep meadows yet, for to forget
The lies, and truths, and pain?....oh! yet
Stands the Church clock at ten to three?
And is there honey still for tea?

Rupert Brooke
(1887–1915)

I Wandered Lonely as a Cloud
Written at Town-end, Grassmere

I wandered lonely as a cloud
That floats on high o'er vales and hills,
When all at once I saw a crowd,
A host, of golden daffodils;
Beside the lake, beneath the trees,
Fluttering and dancing in the breeze.

Continuous as the stars that shine
And twinkle on the milky way,
They stretched in never-ending line
Along the margin of the bay:
Ten thousand saw I at a glance,
Tossing their heads in sprightly dance.

The waves beside them danced; but they
Out-did the sparkling waves in glee:
A poet could not but be gay,
In such a jocund company:
I gazed – and gazed – but little thought
What wealth the show to me had brought:

For oft, when on my couch I lie
In vacant or in pensive mood,
They flash upon that inward eye
Which is the bliss of solitude;
And then my heart with pleasure fills,
And dances with the daffodils.

William Wordsworth
(1770–1850)

In April 1802 William Wordsworth walked round Ullswater with his sister Dorothy. The
flowers he would have seen are the wild daffodil, or Lent lily, with its nodding head and
halo of pale yellow outer petals. Since Wordsworth's time, other kinds of daffodils have
been introduced to Ullswater, so in an effort to conserve the native species, the National
Trust has cleared away the other varieties so that the hillside is a host of the wild flowers,
just as William Wordsworth would have seen it. Wordsworth wrote the poem at Dove
Cottage in Town End, Grasmere.

Home Thoughts from Abroad

I

Oh, to be in England
Now that April's there,
And whoever wakes in England
Sees, some morning, unaware,
That the lowest boughs and brushwood sheaf
Round the elm-tree bole are in tiny leaf,
While the chaffinch sings on the orchard bough
In England – now!

II

And after April, when May follows,
And the whitethroat builds, and all the swallows!
Hark, where my blossomed pear-tree in the hedge
Leans to the field and scatters on the clover
Blossoms and dewdrops – at the bent spray's edge –
That's the wise thrush; he sings each song twice over,
Lest you should think he never could recapture
The first fine careless rapture!
And though the fields look rough with hoary dew
All will be gay when noontide wakes anew
The buttercups, the little children's dower
 – Far brighter than this gaudy melon-flower!

Robert Browning
(1812–1889)

Haymaking

After night's thunder far away had rolled
The fiery day had a kernel sweet of cold,
And in the perfect blue the clouds uncurled,
Like the first gods before they made the world
And misery, swimming the stormless sea
In beauty and in divine gaiety.
The smooth white empty road was lightly strewn
With leaves – the holly's Autumn falls in June –
And fir cones standing up stiff in the heat.
The mill-foot water tumbled white and lit
With tossing crystals, happier than any crowd
Of children pouring out of school aloud.
And in the little thickets where a sleeper
For ever might lie lost, the nettle creeper
And garden-warbler sang unceasingly;
While over them shrill shrieked in his fierce glee
The swift with wings and tail as sharp and narrow
As if the bow had flown off with the arrow.
Only the scent of woodbine and hay new mown
Travelled down the road. In the field sloping down,
Park-like, to where its willows showed the brook,
Haymakers rested. The tosser lay forsook
Out in the sun; and the long waggon stood
Without its team: it seemed it never would
Move from the shadow of that single yew.
The team, as still, until their task was due,
Beside the labourers enjoyed the shade
That three squat oaks mid-field together made
Upon a circle of grass and weed uncut,
And on the hollow, once a chalk pit, but
Now brimmed with nut and elder-flower so clean.
The men leaned on their rakes, about to begin,
But still. And all were silent. All was old,
This morning time, with a great age untold,

Older than Clare and Cobbett, Morland and Crome,
Than, at the field's far edge, the farmer's home,
A white house crouched at the foot of a great tree.
Under the heavens that know not what years be
The men, the beasts, the trees, the implements
Uttered even what they will in times far hence –
All of us gone out of the reach of change –
Immortal in a picture of an old grange.

Edward Thomas
(1878–1917)

To Autumn

I

Season of mists and mellow fruitfulness,
   Close bosom-friend of the maturing sun;
Conspiring with him how to load and bless
   With fruit the vines that round the thatch-eves run;
To bend with apples the moss'd cottage-trees,
   And fill all fruit with ripeness to the core;
     To swell the gourd, and plump, the hazel shells
   With a sweet kernel; to set budding more,
And still more, later flowers for the bees,
Until they think warm days will never cease,
   For Summer has o'er-brimmed their clammy cells.

II

Who hath not seen thee oft amid thy store?
   Sometimes whoever seeks abroad may find
Thee sitting careless on a granary floor,
   Thy hair soft-lifted by the winnowing wind;
Or on a half-reap'd furrow sound asleep,
   Drows'd with the fume of poppies, while thy hook
     Spares the next swathe and all its twined flowers:
And sometimes like a gleaner thou dost keep
   Steady thy laden head across a brook;
   Or by a cyder-press, with patient look,
     Thou watchest the last oozing hours by hours.

III

Where are the songs of Spring? Ay, where are they?
   Think not of them, thou hast thy music too, –
While barred clouds bloom the soft-dying day,
   And touch the stubble-plains with rosy hue;
Then in a wilful choir the small gnats mourn
   Among the river sallows, borne aloft
     Or sinking as the light wind lives or dies;

And full-grown lambs loud bleat from hilly bourn;
    Hedge-crickets sing; and now with treble soft
    The red-breast whistles from a garden-croft;
        And gathering swallows twitter in the skies.

John Keats
(1795–1821)

The Burning of the Leaves

Now is the time for the burning of the leaves.
They go to the fire; the nostril pricks with smoke
Wandering slowly into a weeping mist.
Brittle and blotched, ragged and rotten sheaves!
A flame seizes the smouldering ruin and bites
On stubborn stalks that crackle as they resist.

The last hollyhock's fallen tower is dust;
All the spices of June are a bitter reek,
All the extravagant riches spent and mean.
All burns! The reddest rose is a ghost;
Sparks whirl up, to expire in the mist: the wild
Fingers of fire are making corruption clean.

Now is the time for stripping the spirit bare,
Time for the burning of days ended and done,
Idle solace of things that have gone before:
Rootless hopes and fruitless desires are there;
Let them go to the fire, with never a look behind.
The world that was ours is a world that is ours no more.

They will come again, the leaf and the flower, to arise
From squalor of rottenness into the old splendour,
And magical scents to a wondering memory bring;
The same glory, to shine upon different eyes.
Earth cares for her own ruins, naught for ours.
Nothing is certain, only the certain spring.

Laurence Binyon
(1869–1943)

No!

No sun – no moon!
        No morn – no noon –
No dawn – no dusk – no proper time of day –
        No sky – no earthly view –
        No distance looking blue –
No road – no street – no 't'other side the way' –
        No end to any Row –
        No indications where the Crescents go –
        No top to any steeple –
No recognitions of familiar people –
        No courtesies for showing 'em –
        No knowing 'em! –
No travelling at all – no locomotion,
No inkling of the way – no notion –
        'No go' – by land or ocean –
        No mail – no post –
No news from any foreign coast –
No Park – no Ring – no afternoon gentility –
        No company – no nobility –
No warmth, no cheerfulness, no healthful ease,
        No comfortable feel in any member –
No shade, no shine, no butterflies, no bees,
        No fruits, no flowers, no leaves, no birds, -
        November!

Thomas Hood
(1799–1845)

Stopping by Woods on a Snowy Evening

Whose woods these are I think I know.
His house is in the village though;
He will not see me stopping here
To watch his woods fill up with snow.

My little horse must think it queer
To stop without a farmhouse near
Between the woods and frozen lake
The darkest evening of the year.

He gives his harness bells a shake
To ask if there is some mistake.
The only other sound's the sweep
Of easy wind and downy flake.

The woods are lovely, dark and deep,
But I have promises to keep,
And miles to go before I sleep.
And miles to go before I sleep.

Robert Frost
(1874–1963)

Thaw

Over the land freckled with snow half-thawed
The speculating rooks at their nests cawed
And saw from elm-tops, delicate as flower of grass,
What we below could not see, Winter pass.

Edward Thomas
(1878–1917)

The Garden and Countryside

'The Glimmering Landscape'

Silver

Slowly, silently, now the moon
Walks the night in her silver shoon;
This way, and that, she peers, and sees
Silver fruit upon silver trees;
One by one the casements catch
Her beams beneath the silvery thatch;
Couched in his kennel, like a log,
With paws of silver sleeps the dog;
From their shadowy cote the white breasts peep
Of doves in a silver-feathered sleep;
A harvest mouse goes scampering by,
With silver claws, and silver eye;
And moveless fish in the water gleam,
By silver reeds in a silver stream.

Walter de la Mare
(1873–1956)

Pied Beauty

Glory be to God for dappled things –
    For skies of couple-colour as a brinded cow;
        For rose-moles all in stipple upon trout that swim;
Fresh-firecoal chestnut-falls; finches' wings;
    Landscape plotted and pierced – fold, fallow, and plough;
        And áll trádes, their gear and tackle and trim.

All things counter, original, spare, strange;
    Whatever is fickle, freckled (who knows how?)
        With swift, slow; sweet, sour; adazzle, dim;
He fathers-forth whose beauty is past change:
           Praise him.

Gerard Manley Hopkins
(1844–1889)

The Glory of the Garden

Our England is a garden that is full of stately views,
Of borders, beds and shrubberies and lawns and avenues,
With statues on the terraces and peacocks strutting by;
But the Glory of the Garden lies in more than meets the eye.

For where the old thick laurels grow, along the thin red wall,
You find the tool- and potting-sheds which are the heart of all;
The cold-frames and the hot-houses, the dungpits and the tanks,
The rollers, carts and drain-pipes, with the barrows and the planks.

And there you'll see the gardeners, the men and 'prentice boys
Told off to do as they are bid and do it without noise;
For, except when seeds are planted and we shout to scare the birds,
The Glory of the Garden it abideth not in words.

And some can pot begonias and some can bud a rose,
And some are hardly fit to trust with anything that grows;
But they can roll and trim the lawns and sift the sand and loam,
For the Glory of the Garden occupieth all who come.

Our England is a garden, and such gardens are not made
By singing: – "Oh, how beautiful!" and sitting in the shade,
While better men than we go out and start their working lives
At grubbing weeds from gravel-paths with broken dinner-knives.

There's not a pair of legs so thin, there's not a head so thick,
There's not a hand so weak and white, nor yet a heart so sick,
But it can find some needful job that's crying to be done,
For the Glory of the Garden glorifieth everyone.

Then seek your job with thankfulness and work till further orders,
If it's only netting strawberries or killing slugs in borders;
And when your back stops aching and your hands begin to harden,
You will find yourself a partner in the Glory of the Garden.

Oh, Adam was a gardener, and God who made him sees
That half a proper gardener's work is done upon his knees,
So when your work is finished, you can wash your hands and pray
For the Glory of the Garden, that it may not pass away!
And the Glory of the Garden it shall never pass away!

Rudyard Kipling
(1865–1936)

The Kipling family moved to Bateman's, East Sussex, in 1902 and the poet lived there for
the rest of his life. Much of the garden was laid out according to his design, which still
hangs in the Study. It was designed for fun, as well as beauty, the visitors' book recording
'FIP' by the names of those who fell in the pond.

The Guinea Pig's Garden

We have a little garden,
    A garden of our own,
And every day we water there
    The seeds that we have sown.

We love our little garden,
    And tend it with such care,
You will not find a faded leaf
    Or blighted blossom there.

Beatrix Potter
(1866–1943)

In 1893 Beatrix Potter borrowed her neighbour's guinea pigs so she could paint them.
Nearly thirty years later, while living at Hill Top, her beloved house and retreat in the
Lake District, she completed this poem, which was published in *Cecily Parsley's
Nursery Rhymes*.

The Garden

I

How vainly men themselves amaze
To win the Palm, the Oke or Bayes,
And their uncessant Labours see
Crown'd from some single Herb or Tree,
Whose short and narrow verged Shade
Does prudently their Toyles upbraid,
While all Flow'rs and all Trees do close
To weave the Garlands of repose.

II

Fair quiet, have I found thee here,
And Innocence, thy Sister dear!
Mistaken long, I sought you then
In busie Companies of Men.
Your sacred Plants, if here below,
Only among the Plants will grow.
Society is all but rude,
To this delicious Solitude.

III

No white nor red was ever seen
So am'rous as this lovely green.
Fond Lovers, cruel as their Flame,
Cut in these Trees their Mistress' name.
Little, Alas, they know, or heed,
How far these Beauties Hers exceed!
Fair Trees! where s'ere your barkes I wound,
No Name but shall your own be found.

IV

When we have run our Passions heat,
Love hither makes his best retreat.
The *Gods*, that mortal Beauty chase,
Still in a Tree did end their race.
Apollo hunted *Daphne* so,
Only that She might Laurel grow.
And *Pan* did after *Syrinx* speed,
Not as a Nymph, but for a Reed.

V

What wond'rous Life is this I lead!
Ripe Apples drop about my head;
The Luscious Clusters of the Vine
Upon my Mouth do crush their Wine;
The Nectaren, and curious Peach,
Into my hands themselves do reach;
Stumbling on Melons, as I pass,
Insnar'd with Flow'rs, I fall on Grass.

VI

Mean while the Mind, from pleasures less,
Withdraws into its happiness:
The Mind, that Ocean where each kind
Does streight its own resemblance find,
Yet it creates, transcending these,
Far other Worlds, and other Seas,
Annihilating all that's made
To a green Thought in a green Shade.

VII

Here at the Fountains sliding foot,
Or at some Fruit-tree's mossy root,
Casting the Bodies Vest aside,
My Soul into the boughs does glide:
There like a bird it sits, and sings,
Then whets, and combs its silver Wings;
And, till prepared for longer flight,
Waves in its Plumes the various Light.

VII

Such was that happy Garden-state,
While Man there walk'd without a Mate;
After a Place so pure and sweet,
What other Help could yet be meet!
But 'twas beyond a Mortal's share
To wander solitary there;
Two Paradises 'twere in one
To live in Paradise alone.

IX

How well the skilful Gardener drew
Of flow'rs and herbes this Dial new,
Where from above the milder Sun
Does through a fragrant Zodiack run;
And, as it works, th' industrious Bee
Computes its time as well as we.
How could such sweet and wholesome Hours
Be reckon'd but with herbs and flow'rs!

Andrew Marvell
(1621–1678)

The Garden
Lines 1–65

Small pleasures must correct great tragedies,
Therefore of gardens in the midst of war
I boldly tell. Once of the noble land
I dared to pull the organ stops, the deep
Notes of the bass, the diapason's range
Of rich rotation, yielding crop by crop;
Of season after season as the wheel
Turned cyclic in the grooves and groves of time;
I told the classic tools, the plough, the scythe,
In husbandry's important ritual,
But now of agricultural's little brother
I touch the pretty treble, pluck the string,
Making the necklace of a gardener's year,
A gardener's job, for better or for worse
Strung all too easily in beads of verse.
No strong no ruthless plough-share cutting clods,
No harrow toothèd as the saurian jaws,
Shall tear or comb my sward of garden theme,
But smaller spade and hoe and lowly trowel
And ungloved fingers with their certain touch.

(Delicate are the tools of gardener's craft,
Like a fine woman next a ploughboy set,
But none more delicate than gloveless hand,
That roaming lover of the potting-shed,
That lover soft and tentative, that lover
Desired and seldom found, green-fingered lover
Who scorned to take a woman to his bed.)
So to such small occasions am I fallen,
And in the midst of war,
(Heroic days, when all the pocket folk
Were grabbed and shaken by a larger hand
And lived as they had never lived before
Upon a plane they could not understand

And grasping breathed an atmosphere too rare,
But took it quickly as their native air,
Such big events
That from the slowly opening fount of time
Dripped from the leaky faucet of our days,)
I tried to hold the courage of my ways
In that which might endure,
Daring to find a world in a lost world,
A little world, a little perfect world,
With owlet vision in a blinding time,
And wrote and thought and spoke
These lines, these modest lines, almost demure,
What time the corn stood still in sheaves,
What time the oak
Renewed the million dapple of her leaves.

Yet shall the garden with the state of war
Aptly contrast, a miniature endeavour
To hold the graces and the courtesies
Against a horrid wilderness. The civil
Ever opposed the rude, as centuries'
Slow progress laboured forward, then the check,
Then the slow uphill climb again, the slide
Back to the pit, the climb out of the pit,
Advance, relapse, advance, relapse, advance,
Regular as the measure of a dance;

So does the gardener in a little way
Maintain the bastion of his opposition
And by a symbol keep civility;
So does the brave man strive
To keep enjoyment in his breast alive
When all is dark and even in the heart
Of beauty feels the pallid worm of death.

Vita Sackville-West
(1892–1962)

This poem was started early in 1939 and finally completed after the end of the Second World War. Flower gardens were a luxury in wartime but the garden at Sissinghurst, Kent, continued to bloom in spite of the neglect. Vita Sackville-West wanted the poem to inspire 'courage in adversity' and 'determination to find pleasure and not succumb'. Vita Sackville-West and her husband Harold Nicolson bought Sissinghurst in 1930. She fell in love with it at first sight and created the now-famous garden around the romantic Elizabethan ruins. Part of the attraction of the house was that it was near two of the passions of her life: Knole, her childhood home and Virginia Woolf, who lived at Monk's House, East Sussex.

Domicilium

It faces west, and round the back and sides
High beeches, bending, hang a veil of boughs,
And sweep against the roof. Wild honeysucks
Climb on the walls, and seem to sprout a wish
(If we may fancy wish of trees and plants)
To overtop the apple-trees hard by.

Red roses, lilacs, variegated box
Are there in plenty, and such hardy flowers
As flourish best untrained. Adjoining these
Are herbs and esculents; and farther still
A field; then cottages with trees, and last
The distant hills and sky.

Behind, the scene is wilder. Heath and furze
Are everything that seems to grow and thrive
Upon uneven ground. A stunted thorn
Stands here and there, indeed; and from a pit
An oak uprises, springing from a seed
Dropped by some bird a hundred years ago.

                          In days bygone –
Long gone – my father's mother, who is now
Blest with the blest, would take me out to walk.
At such a time I once inquired of her
How looked the spot when she first settled here.
The answer I remember. 'Fifty years
Have passed since then, my child, and change has marked
The face of all things. Yonder garden-plots
And orchards were uncultivated slopes
O'ergrown with bramble bushes, furze and thorn:
That road a narrow path shut in by ferns,
Which, almost trees, obscured the passer-by.

Our house stood quite alone, and those tall firs
And beeches were not planted. Snakes and efts
Swarmed in the summer days, and nightly bats
Would fly about our bedrooms. Heathcroppers
Lived on the hills, and were our only friends;
So wild it was when we first settled here.'

Thomas Hardy
(1840–1928)

This poem describes the cottage in Higher Brockhampton, Dorset (now known as Hardy's
Cottage), which had been built by Hardy's grandfather and was where the poet was born.
It is one of his first poems and was composed when he was still in his teens.

Elegy Written in a Country Churchyard
Verses 1–9

The curfew tolls the knell of parting day,
The lowing herd wind slowly o'er the lea,
The plowman homeward plods his weary way,
And leaves the world to darkness and to me.

Now fades the glimmering landscape on the sight,
And all the air a solemn stillness holds,
Save where the beetle wheels his droning flight,
And drowsy tinklings lull the distant folds;

Save that from yonder ivy-mantled tow'r
The mopeing owl does to the moon complain
Of such, as wand'ring near her secret bow'r,
Molest her ancient solitary reign.

Beneath those rugged elms, that yew-tree's shade,
Where heaves the turf in many a mould'ring heap,
Each in his narrow cell for ever laid,
The rude Forefathers of the hamlet sleep.

The breezy call of incense-breathing Morn,
The swallow twitt'ring from the straw-built shed,
The cock's shrill clarion, or the ecchoing horn,
No more shall rouse them from their lowly bed.

For them no more the blazing hearth shall burn,
Or busy housewife ply her evening care:
No children run to lisp their sire's return,
Or climb his knees the envied kiss to share.

Oft did the harvest to their sickle yield,
Their furrow oft the stubborn glebe has broke;
How jocund did they drive their team afield!
How bow'd the woods beneath their sturdy stroke!

Let not Ambition mock their useful toil,
Their homely joys, and destiny obscure;
Nor Grandeur hear with a disdainful smile,
The short and simple annals of the poor.

The boast of heraldry, the pomp of power,
And all that beauty, all that wealth e'er gave,
Await alike the inevitable hour.
The paths of glory lead but to the grave.

Thomas Gray
(1716–1771)

The churchyard of this elegy, where Gray is buried, is in Stoke Poges, Buckinghamshire.
Gray's Monument stands near and was commissioned by John Penn and built by James
Wyatt in 1799. Gray's Monument was given to the National Trust in 1925, after Stoke
Poges villagers bought the surrounding land in the 1920s to protect the monument.

Adlestrop

Yes. I remember Adlestrop –
The name, because one afternoon
Of heat the express-train drew up there
Unwontedly. It was late June.

The steam hissed. Someone cleared his throat.
No one left and no one came
On the bare platform. What I saw
Was Adlestrop – only the name

And willows, willow-herb, and grass,
And meadowsweet, and haycocks dry,
No whit less still and lonely fair
Than the high cloudlets in the sky.

And for that minute a blackbird sang
Close by, and round him, mistier,
Farther and farther, all the birds
Of Oxfordshire and Gloucestershire.

Edward Thomas
(1878–1917)

The Anglers Wish

I in these flowry Meads wou'd be:
These Chrystal streams should solace me:
To whose harmonious bubling noise,
I with my Angle wo'd rejoice
Sit here and see the *Turtle-Dove*,
Court his chaste Mate to acts of love,
Or on that bank, feel the west wind
Breath health and plenty, please my mind
To see sweet dew-drops kiss these flowers,
And then, washt off by *April*-showers:
Here hear my *Kenna* sing a song,
There see a Black-bird feed her young,
Or a *Leverock* build her nest;
Here, give my weary spirits rest,
And raise my low pitcht thoughts above
Earth, or what poor mortals love:
> Thus free from *Law-suits*, and the noise
> Of Princes Courts I wou'd rejoyce.

Or with my *Bryan*, and a book,
Loyter long days near *Shawford-brook*;
There sit by him, and eat my meat,
There see the Sun both rise and set:
There bid good morning to next day,
There meditate my time away:
> And angle on, and beg to have
> A quiet passage to a welcome grave.

Izaak Walton
(1593–1683)

Izaak Walton's visits to his friend Charles Cotton's Fishing House on the River Dove, Derbyshire, became the inspiration for his book *The Compleat Angler* (1653). Far more than a simple fishing manual, it includes poetry, literary asides and descriptions of the surrounding countryside. Protected by the National Trust, these 'flowry meads' are now much as Walton would have known them nearly four hundred years ago.

In the Fields

Lord, when I look at lovely things which pass,
　　　Under old trees the shadows of young leaves
Dancing to please the wind along the grass,
　　　Or the gold stillness of the August sun on the August sheaves;
Can I believe there is a heavenlier world than this?
　　　And if there is
Will the strange heart of any everlasting thing
　　　Bring me these dreams that take my breath away?
They come at evening with the home-flying rooks and the scent
　　　of hay,
　　　Over the fields they come. They come in Spring.

Charlotte Mew
(1869–1928)

The Lake Isle of Innisfree

I will arise and go now, and go to Innisfree,
And a small cabin build there, of clay and wattles made:
Nine bean-rows will I have there, a hive for the honey-bee,
And live alone in a bee-loud glade.

And I shall have some peace there, for peace comes dropping slow,
Dropping from the veils of morning to where the cricket sings;
There midnight's all a glimmer, and noon a purple glow,
And evening full of the linnet's wings.

I will arise and go now, for always night and day
I hear lake water lapping with low sounds by the shore;
While I stand on the roadway, or on the pavements grey,
I hear it in the deep heart's core.

W. B. Yeats
(1865–1939)

Beasts and Birds 'Velvet Footsteps'

Leopards at Knole

Leopards on the gable-ends,
Leopards on the painted stair,
Stiff the blazoned shield they bear,
Or and gules, a bend of vair,
Leopards on the gable-ends,
           Leopards everywhere.

Guard and vigil in the night
While the ancient house is sleeping
They three hundred years are keeping,
Nightly from their stations leaping,
Shadows black in moonlight bright,
           Roof to gable creeping.

Rigid when the day returns,
Up aloft in sun or rain
Leopards at their posts again
Watch the shifting pageant's train;
And their jewelled colour burns
           In the window-pane.

Often on the painted stair,
As I passed abstractedly,
Velvet footsteps, two and three,
Padded gravely after me.
– There was nothing, nothing there,
           Nothing there to see.

Vita Sackville-West
(1892–1962)

Vita Sackville-West grew up at Knole and never got over the fact that, as a woman, she
could not inherit the house she loved so much. As you mount the great staircase elegant
leopards perch on the newel posts… possibly waiting to leap down and roam the house
once the visitors have departed.

The Tyger
from: *Songs of Experience*

Tyger Tyger, burning bright,
In the forests of the night:
What immortal hand or eye,
Could frame thy fearful symmetry?

In what distant deeps or skies
Burnt the fire of thine eyes!
On what wings dare he aspire?
What the hand dare seize the fire?

And what shoulder, and what art,
Could twist the sinews of thy heart?
And when thy heart began to beat,
What dread hand? and what dread feet?

What the hammer? what the chain,
In what furnace was thy brain?
What the anvil? what dread grasp,
Dare its deadly terrors clasp?

When the stars threw down their spears
And water'd heaven with their tears:
Did he smile his work to see?
Did he who made the Lamb make thee?

Tyger Tyger, burning bright,
In the forests of the night:
What immortal hand or eye,
Could frame thy fearful symmetry?

William Blake
(1757–1827)

Foal

Darkness is not dark, nor sunlight the light of the sun
But a double journey of insistent silver hooves.
Light wakes in the foal's blind eyes as lightning illuminates corn
With a rustle of fine-eared grass, where a starling shivers.

And whoever watches a foal sees two images,
Delicate, circling, born, the spirit with blind eyes leaping
And the left spirit, vanished, yet here, the vessel of ages
Clay-cold, blue, laid low by her great wide belly the hill.

See him break that circle, stooping to drink, to suck
His mother, vaulted with a beautiful hero's back
Arched under the singing mane,
Shaped to her shining, pricked into awareness
By the swinging dug, amazed by the movement of suns;
His blue fellow has run again down into grass,
And he slips from that mother to the boundless horizons of air,
Looking for that other, the foal no longer there.

But perhaps
In the darkness under the tufted thyme and downtrodden winds,
In the darkness under the violet's roots, in the darkness of the
          pitcher's music,
In the uttermost darkness of a vase
There is still the print of fingers, the shadow of waters.
And under the dry, curled parchment of the soil there is always a
          little foal
Asleep.

So the whole morning he runs here, fulfilling the track
Of so many suns; vanishing the mole's way, moving
Into mole's mysteries under the zodiac,
Racing, stopping in the circle. Startled he stands

Dazzled, where darkness is green, where sunlight is black,
While his mother, grazing, is moving away
From the lagging star of those stars, the unrisen wonder
In the path of the dead, fallen from the sun in her hooves,
And eluding the dead hands, begging him to play.

Vernon Watkins
(1906–1967)

For much of his married life Watkins lived on the Gower peninsula overlooking the
cliffs. Wild ponies roamed the area, their foals running over the fields in spring. There is
a memorial plaque to Watkins at Hunt's Bay, on which are inscribed two lines from his
poem 'Taliesin in Gower'. He is buried at St Mary's Church, Pennard, in South Gower.

Epigram
Engraved on the Collar of a Dog, which I gave to His Royal Highness

I am his Highness' dog at Kew;
Pray tell me, sir, whose dog are you?

Alexander Pope
(1688–1744)

Macavity: The Mystery Cat

Macavity's a Mystery Cat: he's called the Hidden Paw –
For he's a master criminal who can defy the Law.
He's the bafflement of Scotland Yard, the Flying Squad's despair:
For when they reach the scene of crime – *Macavity's not there!*

Macavity, Macavity, there's no one like Macavity,
He's broken every human law, he breaks the law of gravity.
His powers of levitation would make a fakir stare,
And when you reach the scene of crime – *Macavity's not there!*
You may seek him in the basement, you may look up in the air –
But I tell you once and once again, *Macavity's not there!*

Macavity's a ginger cat, he's very tall and thin;
You would know him if you saw him, for his eyes are sunken in.
His brow is deeply lined with thought, his head is highly domed;
His coat is dusty from neglect, his whiskers are uncombed.
He sways his head from side to side, with movements like a snake;
And when you think he's half asleep, he's always wide awake.

Macavity, Macavity, there's no one like Macavity,
For he's a fiend in feline shape, a monster of depravity.
You may meet him in a by-street, you may see him in the square –
But when a crime's discovered, then *Macavity's not there!*

He's outwardly respectable. (They say he cheats at cards.)
And his footprints are not found on any file of Scotland Yard's.
And when the larder's looted, or the jewel-case is rifled,
Or when the milk is missing, or another Peke's been stifled,
Or the greenhouse glass is broken, and the trellis past repair –
Ay, there's the wonder of the thing! *Macavity's not there!*

And when the Foreign Office find a Treaty's gone astray,
Or the Admiralty lose some plans and drawings by the way,
There may be a scrap of paper in the hall or on the stair –
But it's useless to investigate – *Macavity's not there!*
And when the loss has been disclosed, the Secret Service say:
'It *must* have been Macavity!' – but he's a mile away.
You'll be sure to find him resting, or a-licking of his thumbs,
Or engaged in doing complicated long division sums.

Macavity, Macavity, there's no one like Macavity,
There never was a Cat of such deceitfulness and suavity.
He always has an alibi, and one or two to spare:
Whatever time the deed took place – MACAVITY WASN'T
         THERE!
And they say that all the Cats whose wicked deeds are widely known
(I might mention Mungojerrie, I might mention Griddlebone)
Are nothing more than agents for the Cat who all the time
Just controls their operations: the Napoleon of Crime!

T. S. Eliot
(1888–1965)

105

The Owl and the Pussycat

The Owl and the Pussycat went to sea
    In a beautiful pea-green boat,
They took some honey, and plenty of money,
    Wrapped up in a five-pound note.
The Owl looked up to the stars above,
    And sang to a small guitar,
'O lovely Pussy! O Pussy, my love,
    What a beautiful Pussy you are,
        You are,
        You are!
What a beautiful Pussy you are!'

Pussy said to the Owl, 'You elegant fowl!
    How charmingly sweet you sing!
O let us be married! too long we have tarried:
    But what shall we do for a ring?'
They sailed away, for a year and a day,
    To the land where the Bong-tree grows,
And there in a wood a Piggy-wig stood,
With a ring at the end of his nose,
        His nose,
        His nose.
With a ring at the end of his nose.

'Dear Pig, are you willing to sell for one shilling
    Your ring?' Said the Piggy, 'I will.'
So they took it away and were married next day
    By the Turkey who lives on the hill.
They dined on mince, and slices of quince,
    Which they ate with a runcible spoon;

And hand in hand, on the edge of the sand
    They danced by the light of the moon,
        The moon,
        The moon,
They danced by the light of the moon.

Edward Lear
(1812–1888)

To a Skylark

HAIL to thee, blithe Spirit!
      Bird thou never wert,
That from Heaven, or near it,
      Pourest thy full heart
In profuse strains of unpremeditated art.

Higher still and higher
      From the earth thou springest
Like a cloud of fire;
      The blue deep thou wingest,
And singing still dost soar, and soaring ever singest.

In the golden lightning
      Of the sunken sun,
O'er which clouds are bright'ning,
      Thou dost float and run;
Like an unbodied joy whose race is just begun.

The pale purple even
      Melts around thy flight;
Like a star of heaven
      In the broad daylight
Thou art unseen, but yet I hear thy shrill delight,

Keen as are the arrows
      Of that silver sphere,
Whose intense lamp narrows
      In the white dawn clear
Until we hardly see – we feel that it is there.

All the earth and air
        With thy voice is loud,
As, when night is bare,
        From one lonely cloud
The moon rains out her beams, and Heaven is overflowed.

What thou art we know not;
        What is most like thee?
From rainbow clouds there flow not
        Drops so bright to see
As from thy presence showers a rain of melody.

Like a Poet hidden
        In the light of thought,
Singing hymns unbidden,
        Till the world is wrought
To sympathy with hopes and fears it heeded not:

Like a high-born maiden
        In a palace-tower,
Soothing her love-laden
        Soul in secret hour
With music sweet as love, which overflows her bower:

Like a glow-worm golden
        In a dell of dew,
Scattering unbeholden
        Its aëreal hue
Among the flowers and grass, which screen it from the view!

Like a rose embowered
        In its own green leaves,
By warm winds deflowered,
        Till the scent it gives
Makes faint with too much sweet those heavy-wingèd thieves:

Sound of vernal showers
        On the twinkling grass,
Rain-awakened flowers,
        All that ever was
Joyous, and clear, and fresh, thy music doth surpass:

Teach us, Sprite or Bird,
        What sweet thoughts are thine:
I have never heard
        Praise of love or wine
That painted forth a flood of rapture so divine.

Chorus Hymeneal,
        Or triumphal chant,
Matched with thine would be all
        But an empty vaunt,
A thing wherein we feel there is some hidden want.

What objects are the fountains
        Of thy happy strain?
What fields, or waves, or mountains?
        What shapes of sky or plain?
What love of thine own kind? what ignorance of pain?

With thy clear keen joyance
        Languor cannot be:
Shadow of annoyance
        Never came near thee:
Thou lovest – but ne'er knew love's sad satiety.

Walking or asleep,
        Thou of death must deem
Things more true and deep
        Than we mortals dream,
Or how could thy notes flow in such a crystal stream?

We look before and after,
        And pine for what is not:
Our sincerest laughter
        With some pain is fraught;
Our sweetest songs are those that tell of saddest thought.

Yet if we could scorn
        Hate, and pride, and fear;
If we were things born
        Not to shed a tear,
I know not how thy joy we ever should come near.

Better than all measures
        Of delightful sound,
Better than all treasures
        That in books are found,
Thy skill to poet were, thou scorner of the ground!

Teach me half the gladness
        That thy brain must know,
Such harmonious madness
        From my lips would flow
The world should listen then – as I am listening now.

Percy Bysshe Shelley
(1792–1822)

The Raven
Verses 1–8

Once upon a midnight dreary, while I pondered, weak and weary,
Over many a quaint and curious volume of forgotten lore –
While I nodded, nearly napping, suddenly there came a tapping,
As of someone gently rapping, rapping at my chamber door.
''T is some visitor,' I muttered, 'tapping at my chamber door –
                Only this and nothing more.'

Ah, distinctly I remember it was in the bleak December;
And each separate dying ember wrought its ghost upon the floor.
Eagerly I wished the morrow; – vainly I had sought to borrow
From my books surcease of sorrow – sorrow for the lost Lenore –
For the rare and radiant maiden whom the angels name Lenore –
                Nameless *here* for evermore.

And the silken, sad, uncertain rustling of each purple curtain
Thrilled me – filled me with fantastic terrors never felt before;
So that now, to still the beating of my heart, I stood repeating
''T is some visitor entreating entrance at my chamber door –
Some late visitor entreating entrance at my chamber door; –
                This it is and nothing more.'

Presently my soul grew stronger; hesitating then no longer,
'Sir,' I said, 'or Madam, truly your forgiveness I implore;
But the fact is I was napping, and so gently you came rapping,
And so faintly you came tapping, tapping at my chamber door,
That I scarce was sure I heard you' – here I opened wide the door; –
                Darkness there and nothing more.

Deep into that darkness peering, long I stood there wondering, fearing,
Doubting, dreaming dreams no mortal ever dared to dream before;
But the silence was unbroken, and the stillness gave no token,
And the only word there spoken was the whispered word, 'Lenore!'
This I whispered, and an echo murmured back the word 'Lenore!'
                         Merely this and nothing more.

Back into the chamber turning, all my soul within me burning,
Soon again I heard the tapping somewhat louder than before.
'Surely,' said I, 'surely that is someone at my window lattice;
Let me see, then, what thereat is, and this mystery explore –
Let my heart be still a moment and this mystery explore; –
                     'T is the wind and nothing more!'

Open here I flung the shutter, when, with many a flirt and flutter
In there stepped a stately Raven of the saintly days of yore.
Not the least obeisance made he; not a minute stopped or stayed he;
But, with mien of lord or lady, perched above my chamber door –
Perched upon a bust of Pallas just above my chamber door –
                    Perched, and sat, and nothing more.

Then this ebony bird beguiling my sad fancy into smiling,
By the grave and stern decorum of the countenance it wore,
'Thou thy crest be shorn and shaven, thou,' I said, 'are sure no craven,
Ghastly grim and ancient Raven wandering from the Nightly shore –
Tell me what thy lordly name is on the Night's Plutonian shore!'
                  Quoth the Raven, 'Nevermore.'

Edgar Allan Poe
(1809–1849)

Ode to a Nightingale

I

My heart aches, and a drowsy numbness pains
      My sense, as though of hemlock I had drunk,
Or emptied some dull opiate to the drains
      One minute past, and Lethe-wards had sunk:
'Tis not through envy of thy happy lot,
      But being too happy in thine happiness, –
          That thou, light-winged Dryad of the trees,
          In some melodious plot
      Of beechen green, and shadows numberless,
          Singest of summer in full-throated ease.

II

O, for a draught of vintage! that hath been
      Cool'd a long age in the deep-delved earth,
Tasting of Flora and the country green,
      Dance, and Provençal song, and sunburnt mirth!
O for a beaker full of the warm South,
      Full of the true, the blushful Hippocrene,
          With beaded bubbles winking at the brim,
          And purple-stained mouth;
      That I might drink, and leave the world unseen,
          And with thee fade away into the forest dim:

III

Fade far away, dissolve, and quite forget
      What thou among the leaves hast never known,
The weariness, the fever, and the fret
      Here, where men sit and hear each other groan;
Where palsy shakes a few, sad, last grey hairs,
      Where youth grows pale, and spectre-thin, and dies;
          Where but to think is to be full of sorrow
          And leaden-eyed despairs,
      Where Beauty cannot keep her lustrous eyes,
          Or new Love pine at them beyond to-morrow

IV

Away! away! for I will fly to thee,
    Not charioted by Bacchus and his pards,
But on the viewless wings of Poesy,
    Though the dull brain perplexes and retards:
Already with thee! tender is the night,
    And haply the Queen-Moon is on her throne,
        Cluster'd around by all her starry Fays;
            But here there is no light,
    Save what from heaven is with the breezes blown
        Through verdurous glooms and winding mossy ways.

V

I cannot see what flowers are at my feet,
    Nor what soft incense hangs upon the boughs,
But, in embalmed darkness, guess each sweet
    Wherewith the seasonable month endows
The grass, the thicket, and the fruit-tree wild;
    White hawthorn, and the pastoral eglantine;
        Fast fading violets cover'd up in leaves;
            And mid-May's eldest child,
    The coming musk-rose, full of dewy wine,
        The murmurous haunt of flies on summer eves.

VI

Darkling I listen; and, for many a time
    I have been half in love with easeful Death,
Call'd him soft names in many a mused rhyme,
    To take into the air my quiet breath;
Now more than ever seems it rich to die,
    To cease upon the midnight with no pain,
        While thou art pouring forth thy soul abroad
            In such an ecstasy!
    Still would'st thou sing, and I have ears in vain –
        To thy high requiem become a sod.

VII

Thou wast not born for death, immortal Bird!
No hungry generations tread thee down;
The voice I hear this passing night was heard
In ancient days by emperor and clown:
Perhaps the self same song that found a path
Through the sad heart of Ruth, when, sick for home,
She stood in tears amid the alien corn;
The same that oft-times hath
Charm'd magic casements, opening on the foam
Of perilous seas, in faery lands forlorn.

VIII

Forlorn! the very word is like a bell
To toll me back from thee to my sole self!
Adieu! the fancy cannot cheat so well
As she is fam'd to do, deceiving elf.
Adieu! adieu! thy plaintive anthem fades
Past the near meadows, over the still stream,
Up the hill-side; and now 'tis buried deep
In the next valley-glades:
Was it a vision, or a waking dream?
Fled is that music: – Do I wake or sleep?

John Keats
(1795–1821)

The Sea

'Along the

Sand'

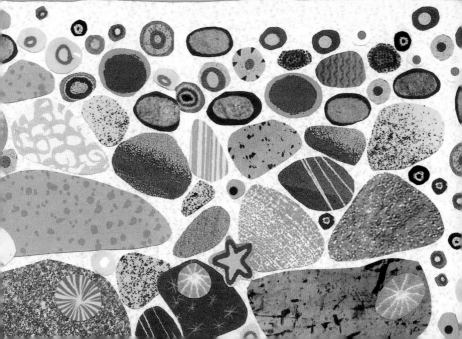

Exultation is the Going

Exultation is the going
Of an inland soul to sea,
Past the houses – past the headlands –
Into deep Eternity –

Bred as we, among the mountains,
Can the sailor understand
The divine intoxication
Of the first league out from land?

Emily Dickinson
(1830–1886)

Ariel's Song
from: *The Tempest*, Act I, Scene ii

Full fathom five thy father lies;
      Of his bones are coral made;
Those are pearls that were his eyes:
      Nothing of him that doth fade
But doth suffer a sea-change
Into something rich and strange
Sea-nymphs hourly ring his knell:
            Ding-dong.
Hark! now I hear them.
            Ding-dong, bell.

William Shakespeare
(1564–1616)

Glanmore Sonnets: VII

Dogger, Rockall, Malin, Irish Sea:
Green, swift upsurges, North Atlantic flux
Conjured by that strong gale-warning voice
Collapse into a silent penumbra.
Midnight and closedown. Sirens of the tundra,
Of eel-road, seal-road, keel-road, whale-road, raise
Their wind-compounded keen behind the baize
And drive the trawlers to the lee of Wicklow.
L'Etoile, *Le Guillemot*, *La Belle Hélène*
Nursed their bright names this morning in the bay
That toiled like mortar. It was marvellous
And actual, I said out loud, 'A haven,'
The word deepening, clearing, like the sky
Elsewhere on Minches, Cromarty, The Faroes.

Seamus Heaney
(1939–2013)

Cargoes

Quinquireme of Nineveh from distant Ophir
Rowing home to haven in sunny Palestine,
With a cargo of ivory,
And apes and peacocks,
Sandalwood, cedarwood, and sweet white wine.

Stately Spanish galleon coming from the Isthmus,
Dipping through the Tropics by the palm-green shores,
With a cargo of diamonds,
Emeralds, amethysts,
Topazes, and cinnamon, and gold moidores.

Dirty British coaster with a salt-caked smoke stack
Butting through the Channel in the mad March days,
With a cargo of Tyne coal,
Road-rail, pig-lead,
Firewood, iron-ware, and cheap tin trays.

John Masefield
(1878–1967)

Sonnet LXXV
from: *Amoretti*

One day I wrote her name upon the strand,
  But came the waves and washed it away:
  Again I wrote it with a second hand,
  But came the tide and made my pains his prey.
Vain man, said she, that dost in vain assay,
  A mortal thing so to immortalize
  For I myself shall like to this decay,
  And eke my name be wiped out likewise.

Not so (quod I) let baser things devise
  To die in dust, but you shall live by fame:
  My verse your virtues rare shall eternize,
  And in the heavens write your glorious name:
Where whereas Death shall all the world subdue,
  Our love shall live, and later life renew.

Edmund Spenser
(*c.* 1552–1599)

A Smuggler's Song
from: 'Hal o' the Draft' in *Puck of Pook's Hill*

If you wake at midnight, and hear a horse's feet,
Don't go drawing back the blind, or looking in the street,
Them that asks no questions isn't told a lie.
Watch the wall, my darling, while the Gentlemen go by!
        Five and twenty ponies
        Trotting through the dark –
        Brandy for the Parson,
        'Baccy for the Clerk;
        Laces for a lady, letters for a spy,
And watch the wall, my darling, while the Gentlemen go by!

Running round the woodlump if you chance to find
Little barrels, roped and tarred, all full of brandy-wine,
Don't you shout to come and look, nor use 'em for your play.
Put the brishwood back again – and they'll be gone next day!

If you see the stable-door setting open wide;
If you see a tired horse lying down inside;
If your mother mends a coat cut about and tore;
If the lining's wet and warm – don't you ask no more!

If you meet King George's men, dressed in blue and red,
You be careful what you say, and mindful what is said.
If they call you "pretty maid" and chuck you 'neath the chin,
Don't you tell where no one is, nor yet where no one's been!

Knocks and footsteps round the house – whistles after dark –
You've no call for running out till the house-dogs bark.
Trusty's here, and *Pincher's* here, and see how dumb they lie –
They don't fret to follow when the Gentlemen go by!

If you do as you've been told, 'likely there's a chance,
You'll be give a dainty doll, all the way from France,
With a cap of Valenciennes, and a velvet hood –
A present from the Gentlemen, along o' being good!
        Five and twenty ponies
        Trotting through the dark –
        Brandy for the Parson,
        'Baccy for the Clerk;
Them that asks no questions isn't told a lie –
Watch the wall, my darling, while the Gentlemen go by!

Rudyard Kipling
(1865–1936)

Puck of Pook's Hill consists of a collection of short stories told to two children, Dan and
Una. Dan was the same age as Kipling's son John so it is likely he wrote the stories for
his children. They are a delightful mixture of history and archaeology, with a little magic
added, and describe the area round Bateman's where the Kiplings lived.

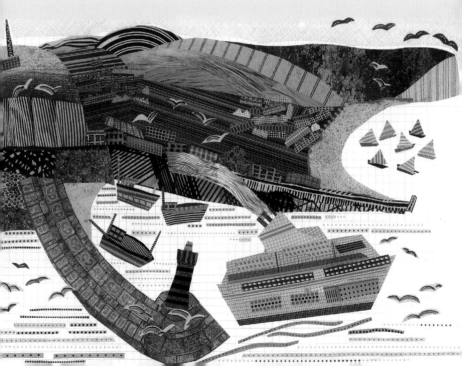

Neither Out Far, Nor in Deep

The people along the sand
All turn and look one way.
They turn their back on the land.
They look at the sea all day.

As long as it takes to pass
A ship keeps raising its hull;
The wetter ground like glass
Reflects a standing gull.

The land may vary more;
But wherever the truth may be –
The water comes ashore,
And the people look at the sea.

They cannot look out far.
They cannot look in deep.
But when was that ever a bar
To any watch they keep?

Robert Frost
(1874–1963)

Not Waving but Drowning

Nobody heard him, the dead man,
But still he lay moaning:
I was much further out than you thought
And not waving but drowning.

Poor chap, he always loved larking
And now he's dead
It must have been too cold for him his heart gave way,
They said.

Oh, no no no, it was too cold always
(Still the dead one lay moaning)
I was much too far out all my life
And not waving but drowning.

Stevie Smith
(1902–1971)

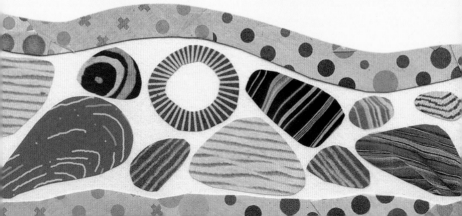

Casabianca

The boy stood on the burning deck,
    Whence all but him had fled;
The flame that lit the battle's wreck
    Shone round him o'er the dead.

Yet beautiful and bright he stood,
    As born to rule the storm;
A creature of heroic blood,
    A proud though childlike form.

The flames roll'd on – he would not go
    Without his father's word;
That father, faint in death below,
    His voice no longer heard.

He call'd aloud, "Say, father, say,
    If yet my task is done?"
He knew not that the chieftain lay
    Unconscious of his son.

"Speak, father!" once again he cried,
    "If I may yet be gone!"
And but the booming shots replied,
    And fast the flames rolled on.

Upon his brow he felt their breath,
    And in his waving hair;
And looked from the lone post of death
    In still, yet brave despair;

And shouted but once more aloud,
    "My father! must I stay?"
While o'er him fast, through sail and shroud,
    The wreathing fires made way.

They wrapt the ship in splendour wild,
      They caught the flag on high,
And stream'd above the gallant child
      Like banners in the sky.

There came a burst of thunder sound –
      The boy – Oh! where was he?
– Ask of the winds, that far around
      With fragment strewed the sea;

With mast, and helm, and pennon fair,
      That well had borne their part –
But the noblest thing that perished there
      Was that young, faithful heart.

Felicia Dorothea Hemans
(1793–1835)

The Rime of the Ancient Mariner
Part I

It is an ancient Mariner,
And he stoppeth one of three.
'By thy long grey beard and glittering eye,
Now wherefore stopp'st thou me?

The Bridegroom's doors are opened wide,
And I am next of kin;
The guests are met, the feast is set:
May'st hear the merry din.'

He holds him with his skinny hand,
'There was a ship,' quoth he.
'Hold off! unhand me, grey-beard loon!'
Eftsoons his hand dropt he.

He holds him with his glittering eye –
The Wedding-Guest stood still,
And listens like a three years' child:
The Mariner hath his will.

The Wedding-Guest sat on a stone:
He cannot choose but hear;
And thus spake on that ancient man,
The bright-eyed Mariner.

'The ship was cheered, the harbour cleared,
Merrily did we drop
Below the kirk, below the hill,
Below the lighthouse top.

The Sun came up upon the left,
Out of the sea came he!
And he shone bright, and on the right
Went down into the sea.

Higher and higher every day,
Till over the mast at noon – '
The Wedding-Guest here beat his breast
For he heard the loud bassoon.

The bride hath paced into the hall,
Red as a rose is she;
Nodding their heads before her goes
They merry minstrelsy.

The Wedding-Guest he beat his breast,
Yet he cannot choose but hear;
And thus spake on that ancient man,
The bright-eyed Mariner.

'And now the Storm-blast came, and he
Was tyrannous and strong:
He struck with o'ertaking wings
And chased us south along.

With sloping masts and dipping prow,
As who pursued with yell and blow
Still treads the shadow of his foe,
And forward leads his head,
The ship drove fast, loud roared the blast,
And southward aye we fled.

And now there came both mist and snow,
And it grew wondrous cold:
And ice, mast-high, came floating by,
As green as emerald.

And through the drifts the snowy clifts
Did send a dismal sheen;
Nor shapes of men nor beasts we ken –
The ice was all between.

The ice was here, the ice was there,
The ice was all around:
It cracked and growled, and roared and howled,
Like noises in a swound!

At length did cross an Albatross,
Thorough the fog it came;
As if it had been a Christian soul,
We hailed it in God's name.

It ate the food it ne'er had eat,
And round and round it flew.
The ice did split with a thunder-fit;
The helmsman steered us through!

And a good south wind sprung up behind;
The Albatross did follow,
And every day, for food or play,
Came to the mariner's hollo!

In mist or cloud, on mast or shroud,
It perched for vespers nine;
Whiles all the night, through fog-smoke white,
Glimmered the white Moon-shine.'

'God save thee, ancient Mariner!
From the fiends, that plague thee thus! –
Why look'st thou so?' With my cross-bow
I shot the Albatross.

Samuel Taylor Coleridge
(1772–1834)

Coleridge lived in the village of Nether Stowey, Somerset, at the house now known as
Coleridge Cottage for three years from 1797. During this time he produced many of his
finest works including 'The Rime of the Ancient Mariner'. While there he frequently
went walking in the Quantock Hills with Wordsworth. Together they planned to write a
ballad based on the committing of a crime and Wordsworth suggested the shooting of an
albatross. In the end Coleridge wrote the poem on his own.

Dover Beach

The sea is calm tonight.
The tide is full, the moon lies fair
Upon the straits; – on the French coast the light
Gleams and is gone; the cliffs of England stand,
Glimmering and vast, out in the tranquil bay.
Come to the window, sweet is the night air!
Only, from the long line of spray
Where the sea meets the moon-blanch'd land,
Listen! you hear the grating roar
Of pebbles which the waves draw back, and fling,
At their return, up the high strand,
Begin, and cease, and then again begin,
With tremulous cadence slow, and bring
The eternal note of sadness in.

Sophocles long ago
Heard it on the Ægæan, and it brought
Into his mind the turbid ebb and flow
Of human misery; we
Find also in the sound a thought,
Hearing it by this distant northern sea.

The Sea of Faith
Was once, at the full, and round earth's shore
Lay like the folds of a bright girdle furl'd.
But now I only hear
Its melancholy, long, withdrawing roar,
Retreating, to the breath
Of the night-wind, down the vast edges drear
And naked shingles of this world.

Ah, love, let us be true
To one another! for the world, which seems
To lie before us like a land of dreams,

So various, so beautiful, so new,
Hath really neither joy, nor love, nor light,
Nor certitude, nor peace, nor help for pain;
And we are here as on a darkling plain
Swept with confused alarms of struggle and flight,
Where ignorant armies clash by night.

Matthew Arnold
(1822–1888)

Twenty thousand years ago the towering chalk cliffs at Dover were joined to France. Now there are spectacular cliff-top walks, a wealth of fascinating history to unearth and, on a clear day, a breathtaking view across the Channel. The National Trust now looks after the White Cliffs of Dover for future generations to enjoy.

Journeys

'I Travelled among Unknown Men'

The General Prologue

from: *The Canterbury Tales*, lines 1–18

> Whan that Aprill with his shourés soote
> The droghte of March hath perced to the roote,
> And bathed every veyne in swich licour
> Of which vertu engendred is the flour;
> Whan Zephirus eek with his sweeté breeth
> Inspired hath in every holt and heeth
> The tendre croppés, and the yongé sonne
> Hath in the Ram his halvé cours yronne,
> And smalé fowelés maken melodye,
> That slepen al the nyght with open ye
> (So priketh hem nature in hir corages);
> Thanne longen folk to goon on pilgrimages,
> And palmerés for to seken straunge strondes,
> To ferné halwes, kowthe in sondry londes;
> And specially from every shires ende
> Of Engelond to Caunterbury they wende,
> The hooly blisful martir for to seke,
> That hem hath holpen whan that they were seeke.

Geoffrey Chaucer
(*c.* 1343–1400)

The Highwayman
Part One

I

The wind was a torrent of darkness among the gusty trees.
The moon was a ghostly galleon tossed upon cloudy seas.
The road was a ribbon of moonlight over the purple moor,
And the highwayman came riding –

    Riding – riding –

The highwayman came riding, up to the old inn-door.

II

He'd a French cocked-hat on his forehead, a bunch of lace at his chin,
A coat of the claret velvet, and breeches of brown doe-skin
They fitted with never a wrinkle. His boots were up to the thigh.
And he rode with a jewelled twinkle,

    His pistol butts a-twinkle,

His rapier hilt a-twinkle, under the jewelled sky.

III

Over the cobbles he clattered and clashed in the dark inn-yard.
He tapped with his whip on the shutters, but all was locked
    and barred.
He whistled a tune to the window, and who should be waiting there
But the landlord's black-eyed daughter,

    Bess, the landlord's daughter,

Plaiting a dark red love-knot into her long black hair.

IV

And dark in the dark old inn-yard a stable-wicket creaked
Where Tim the ostler listened. His face was white and peaked.
His eyes were hollows of madness, his hair like mouldy hay,
But he loved the landlord's daughter,

    The landlord's red-lipped daughter.

Dumb as a dog he listened, and he heard the robber say –

V

"One kiss, my bonny sweetheart, I'm after a prize to-night,
But I shall be back with the yellow gold before the morning light;
Yet, if they press me sharply, and harry me through the day,
Then look for me by moonlight,
  Watch for me by moonlight,
I'll come to thee by moonlight, though hell should bar the way."

VI

He rose up in the stirrups. He scarce could reach her hand,
But she loosened her hair in the casement. His face burnt like a brand
As the black cascade of perfume came tumbling over his breast;
And he kissed its waves in the moonlight
  (Oh, sweet black waves in the moonlight!)
Then he tugged at his rein in the moonlight, and galloped away to
  the west.

Alfred Noyes
(1880–1958)

Sea-Fever

I must go down to the seas again, to the lonely sea and the sky,
And all I ask is a tall ship and a star to steer her by,
And the wheel's kick and the wind's song and the white sail's shaking,
And a grey mist on the sea's face and a grey dawn breaking.

I must go down to the seas again, for the call of the running tide
Is a wild call and a clear call that may not be denied;
And all I ask is a windy day with the white clouds flying,
And the flung spray and the blown spume, and the sea-gulls crying.

I must go down to the seas again, to the vagrant gypsy life,
To the gull's way and the whale's way where the wind's like a
        whetted knife;
And all I ask is a merry yarn from a laughing fellow-rover,
And a quiet sleep and a sweet dream when the long trick's over.

John Masefield
(1878–1967)

London

Athwart the sky a lowly sigh
        From west to east the sweet wind carried;
The sun stood still on Primrose Hill;
        His light in all the city tarried:
The clouds on viewless columns bloomed
Like smouldering lilies unconsumed.

'Oh sweetheart, see! how shadowy,
        Of some occult magician's rearing,
Or swung in space of heaven's grace
        Dissolving, dimly reappearing,

Afloat upon ethereal tides
St. Paul's above the city rides!'

A rumour broke through the thin smoke
        Enwreathing abbey, tower, and palace,
The parks, the squares, the thoroughfares,
        The million-peopled lanes and alleys,
An ever-muttering prisoned storm,
The heart of London beating warm.

John Davidson
(1857–1909)

Composed Upon Westminster Bridge
September 3, 1802
Written on the roof of a coach, on my way to France.

Earth has not anything to show more fair:
Dull would he be of soul who could pass by
A sight so touching in its majesty:
This City now doth, like a garment, wear
The beauty of the morning; silent, bare,
Ships, towers, domes, theatres, and temples lie
Open unto the fields, and to the sky;
All bright and glittering in the smokeless air.
Never did sun more beautifully steep
In his first splendour, valley, rock, or hill;
Ne'er saw I, never felt, a calm so deep!
The river glideth at his own sweet will:
Dear God! the very houses seem asleep;
And all that mighty heart is lying still!

William Wordsworth
(1770–1850)

Journey of the Magi

'A cold coming we had of it,
Just the worst time of the year
For a journey, and such a long journey:
The ways deep and the weather sharp,
The very dead of winter.'
And the camels galled, sore-footed, refractory,
Lying down in the melting snow.
There were times we regretted
The summer palaces on slopes, the terraces,
And the silken girls bringing sherbet.
Then the camel men cursing and grumbling
And running away, and wanting their liquor and women,
And the night-fires going out, and the lack of shelters,
And the cities hostile and the towns unfriendly
And the villages dirty and charging high prices:
A hard time we had of it.
At the end we preferred to travel all night
Sleeping in snatches,
With the voices singing in our ears, saying
That this was all folly.

Then at dawn we came to a temperate valley,
Wet, below the snow line, smelling of vegetation,
With a running stream and a water-mill beating the darkness,
And three trees on the low sky.
And an old white horse galloped away in the meadow.
Then we came to a tavern with vine-leaves over the lintel,
Six hands at an open door dicing for pieces of silver,
And feet kicking the empty wine-skins.
But there was no information, and so we continued
And arrived at evening, not a moment too soon
Finding the place; it was (you may say) satisfactory.

All this was a long time ago, I remember,
And I would do it again, but set down
This set down
This: were we led all that way for
Birth or Death? There was a Birth, certainly
We had evidence and no doubt. I had seen birth and death,
But had thought they were different; this Birth was
Hard and bitter agony for us, like Death, our death.
We returned to our places, these Kingdoms,
But no longer at ease here, in the old dispensation,
With an alien people clutching their gods.
I should be glad of another death.

T. S. Eliot
(1888–1965)

The Road Not Taken

Two roads diverged in a yellow wood,
And sorry I could not travel both
And be one traveller, long I stood
And looked down one as far as I could
To where it bent in the undergrowth;

Then took the other, as just as fair,
And having perhaps the better claim,
Because it was grassy and wanted wear;
Though as for that the passing there
Had worn them really about the same,

And both that morning equally lay
In leaves no step had trodden black.
Oh, I kept the first for another day!
Yet knowing how way leads on to way,
I doubted if I should ever come back.

I shall be telling this with a sigh
Somewhere ages and ages hence:
Two roads diverged in a wood, and I –
I took the one less travelled by,
And that has made all the difference.

Robert Frost
(1874–1963)

I Travelled Among Unknown Men

I travelled among unknown men,
    In lands beyond the sea;
Nor, England! did I know till then
    What love I bore to thee.

'Tis past, that melancholy dream!
    Nor will I quit thy shore
A second time; for still I seem
    To love thee more and more.

Among thy mountains did I feel
    The joy of my desire;
And she I cherished turned her wheel
    Beside an English fire.

Thy mornings showed, thy nights concealed
    The bowers where Lucy played;
And thine is, too, the last green field
    Which Lucy's eyes surveyed.

William Wordsworth
(1770–1850)

The Listeners

'Is there anybody there?' said the Traveller,
      Knocking on the moonlit door;
And his horse in the silence champed the grasses
      Of the forest's ferny floor:
And a bird flew up out of the turret,
      Above the Traveller's head:
And he smote upon the door again a second time;
      'Is there anybody there?' he said.
But no one descended to the Traveller;
      No head from the leaf-fringed sill
Leaned over and looked into his grey eyes,
      Where he stood perplexed and still.
But only a host of phantom listeners
      That dwelt in the lone house then
Stood listening in the quiet of the moonlight
      To that voice from the world of men:
Stood thronging the faint moonbeams on the dark stair,
      That goes down to the empty hall,
Hearkening in an air stirred and shaken
      By the lonely Traveller's call.
And he felt in his heart their strangeness,
      And their stillness answering his cry,
While his horse moved, cropping the dark turf,
      'Neath the starred and leafy sky;
For he suddenly smote on the door, even
      Louder and lifted his head: –
'Tell them I came, and no one answered,
      That I kept my word,' he said.
Never the least stir made the listeners,
      Though every word he spake
Fell echoing through the shadowiness of the still house

From the one man left awake:
Ay, they heard his foot upon the stirrup,
        And the sound of iron on stone,
And how the silence surged softly backward,
        When the plunging hoofs were gone.

Walter de la Mare
(1873–1956)

The Roman Road

The Roman Road runs straight and bare
As the pale parting-line in hair
Across the heath. And thoughtful men
Contrast its days of Now and Then
And delve, and measure, and compare;

Visioning on the vacant air
Helmed legionaries, who proudly rear
The Eagle, as they pace again
    The Roman Road.

But no tall brass-helmed legionnaire
Haunts it for me. Uprises there
A mother's form upon my ken,
Guiding my infant steps, as when
We walked that ancient thoroughfare,
    The Roman Road.

Thomas Hardy
(1840–1928)

The Rolling English Road

Before the Roman came to Rye or out to Severn strode,
The rolling English drunkard made the rolling English road.
A reeling road, a rolling road, that rambles round the shire,
And after him the parson ran, the sexton and the squire;
A merry road, a mazy road, and such as we did tread
The night we went to Birmingham by way of Beachy Head.

I knew no harm of Bonaparte and plenty of the Squire,
And for to fight the Frenchman I did not much desire;
But I did bash their baggonets because they came arrayed
To straighten out the crooked road an English drunkard made,
Where you and I went down the lane with ale-mugs in our hands,
The night we went to Glastonbury by way of Goodwin Sands.

His sins they were forgiven him; or why do flowers run
Behind him; and the hedges all strengthening in the sun?
The wild thing went from left to right and knew not which was which,
But the wild rose was above him when they found him in the ditch.
God pardon us, nor harden us; we did not see so clear
The night we went to Bannockburn by way of Brighton Pier.

My friends, we will not go again or ape an ancient rage,
Or stretch the folly of our youth to be the shame of age,
But walk with clearer eyes and ears this path that wandereth,
And see undrugged in evening light the decent inn of death;
For there is good news yet to hear and fine things to be seen,
Before we go to Paradise by way of Kensal Green.

G. K. Chesterton
(1874–1936)

The Way Through the Woods

They shut the road through the woods
Seventy years ago.
Weather and rain have undone it again,
And now you would never know
There was once a road through the woods
Before they planted the trees.
It is underneath the coppice and heath
And the thin anemones.
Only the keeper sees
That, where the ring-dove broods,
And the badgers roll at ease,
There was once a road through the woods.

Yet, if you enter the woods
Of a summer evening late,
When the night-air cools on the trout-ringed pools
Where the otter whistles his mate,
(They fear not men in the woods,
Because they see so few.)
You will hear the beat of a horse's feet,
And the swish of a skirt in the dew,
Steadily cantering through
The misty solitudes,
As though they perfectly knew
The old lost road through the woods. . . .
But there is no road through the woods.

Rudyard Kipling
(1865–1936)

Behind Bateman's, the River Dudwell flows through a valley which gave Kipling the
inspiration for many of his most magical stories and poems. Some of the paths are now
grown over, but others are just as Kipling would have walked them nearly a century ago.

War

'The Noise of Battle'

Morte d'Arthur
Lines 1–44

So all day long the noise of battle roll'd
Among the mountains by the winter sea;
Until King Arthur's table, man by man,
Had fallen in Lyonnesse about their Lord,
King Arthur: then, because his wound was deep,
The bold Sir Bedivere uplifted him,
Sir Bedivere, the last of all his knights,
And bore him to a chapel nigh the field,
A broken chancel with a broken cross,
That stood on a dark straight of barren land.
On one side lay the Ocean, and on one
Lay a great water, and the moon was full.

Then spake King Arthur to Sir Bedivere:
'The sequel of to-day unsolders all
The goodliest fellowship of famous knights
Whereof this world holds record. Such a sleep
They sleep – the men I loved. I think that we
Shall never more, at any future time,
Delight our souls with talk of knightly deeds,
Walking about the gardens and the halls
Of Camelot, as in the days that were.
I perish by this people which I made, –
Tho' Merlin sware that I should come again
To rule once more – but let what will be, be,
I am so deeply smitten thro' the helm
That without help I cannot last till morn,
Thou therefore take my brand Excalibur,
Which was my pride: for thou rememberest how
In those old days, one summer noon, an arm
Rose up from out the bosom of the lake,
Clothed in white samite, mystic, wonderful,
Holding the sword – and how I row'd across
And took it, and have worn it, like a king:

And, wheresoever I am sung or told
In aftertime, this also shall be known:
But now delay not; take Excalibur,
And fling him far into the middle mere:
Watch what thou seëst, and lightly bring me word.'

       To him replied the bold Sir Bedivere:
'It is not meet, Sir King, to leave thee thus,
Aidless, alone, and smitten thro' the helm.
A little thing may harm a wounded man.
Yet I thy hest will all perform at full,
Watch what I see, and lightly bring thee word.'

Alfred, Lord Tennyson
(1809–1892)

The place to which Sir Bedevere takes King Arthur is Loe Pool, near Lizard Point.
Here Cornwall's largest freshwater lake meets the sea at the shingle bank of Loe Bar,
the barren place in the poem between the Ocean and the great water. Lizard Point is the
southernmost place in Britain and is looked after by the National Trust.

The Charge of the Light Brigade

I

Half a league, half a league,
  Half a league onward,
All in the valley of Death
  Rode the six hundred.
'Forward, the Light Brigade!
Charge for the guns!' he said:
Into the valley of Death
  Rode the six hundred.

II

'Forward, the Light Brigade!'
Was there a man dismay'd?
Not tho' the soldier knew
  Some one had blunder'd:
Their's not to make reply,
Their's not to reason why,
Their's but to do and die:
Into the valley of Death
  Rode the six hundred.

III

Cannon to the right of them,
Cannon to the left of them,
Cannon in front of them
  Volley'd and thunder'd;
Storm'd at with shot and shell,
Boldly they rode and well,
Into the jaws of Death,
 Into the mouth of Hell
  Rode the six hundred.

IV

Flash'd all their sabres bare,
Flash'd as they turn'd in air
Sabring the gunners there,
Charging the army, while
   All the world wonder'd:
Plunged in the battery-smoke
Right thro' the line they broke;
Cossack and Russian
Reel'd from the sabre-stroke
   Shatter'd and sunder'd.
Then they rode back, but not
   Not the six hundred.

V

Cannon to the right of them,
Cannon to the left of them,
Cannon behind them
   Volley'd and thunder'd;
Storm'd at with shot and shell,
While horse and hero fell,
They that had fought so well
Came thro' the jaws of Death,
Back from the mouth of Hell,
All that was left of them,
   Left of six hundred.

VI

When can their glory fade?
O the wild charge they made!
   All the world wonder'd.
Honour the charge they made!
Honour the Light Brigade,
   Noble six hundred!

Alfred, Lord Tennyson
(1809–1892)

The General

'Good-morning; good-morning!' the General said
When we met him last week on our way to the line.
Now the soldiers he smiled at are most of 'em dead,
And we're cursing his staff for incompetent swine.
'He's a cheery old card,' grunted Harry to Jack
As they slogged up to Arras with rifle and pack.

.   .   .   .   .

But he did for them both by his plan of attack.

Siegfried Sassoon
(1886–1967)

1914: V The Soldier

If I should die, think only this of me:
  That there's some corner of a foreign field
That is for ever England. There shall be
  In that rich earth a richer dust concealed;
A dust whom England bore, shaped, made aware,
  Gave, once, her flowers to love, her ways to roam,
A body of England's, breathing English air,
  Washed by the rivers, blest by the suns of home.

And think, this heart, all evil shed away,
  A pulse in the eternal mind, no less
    Gives somewhere back the thoughts by England given;
Her sights and sounds; dreams happy as her day;
  And laughter, learnt of friends; and gentleness,
    In hearts at peace, under an English heaven.

Rupert Brooke
(1887–1915)

Dulce Et Decorum Est

Bent double, like old beggars under sacks,
Knock-kneed, coughing like hags, we cursed through sludge,
Till on the haunting flares we turned our backs
And towards our distant rest began to trudge.
Men marched asleep. Many had lost their boots
But limped on, blood-shod. All went lame; all blind;
Drunk with fatigue; deaf even to the hoots
Of tired, outstripped Five-Nines that dropped behind.

Gas! Gas! Quick, boys! – An ecstasy of fumbling,
Fitting the clumsy helmets just in time;
But someone still was yelling out and stumbling
And flound'ring like a man in fire or lime. . .
Dim, through the misty panes and thick green light,
As under a green sea, I saw him drowning.

In all my dreams, before my helpless sight,
He plunges at me, guttering, choking, drowning.

If in some smothering dreams you too could pace
Behind the wagon that we flung him in,
And watch the white eyes writhing in his face,
His hanging face, like a devil's sick of sin;
If you could hear, at every jolt, the blood
Come gargling from the froth-corrupted lungs,
Obscene as cancer, bitter as the cud
Of vile, incurable sores on innocent tongues, –
My friend, you would not tell us with such high zest
To children ardent for some desperate glory,
The old Lie: Dulce et decorum est
Pro patria mori.

Wilfred Owen
(1893–1918)

Toasts and Memories
(To the Men of the 2/5 Gloucester Regiment)

When once I sat in estaminets
    With trusty friends of mine,
We drank to folk in England
    And pledged them well in wine,

While thoughts of Gloucester filled us –
    Roads against windy skies
At sunset, Severn river,
    Red inn-blinds, country cries.

That stung the heart with sorrow
    And barbéd sweet delight
At Riez Bailleul, Laventie,
    At Merville, many a night.

Now I am over Channel
    I cannot help but think
Of friends who stifle longing
    With friendly food and drink.

"Where's Gurney now, I wonder,
    That smoked a pipe all day;
Sometimes that talked like blazes,
    Sometimes had naught to say?"

And I, at home, must wonder
    Where all my comrades are:
Those men whose Heart-of-Beauty
    Was never strained by War.

Ivor Gurney
(1890–1937)

The manuscript of this poem was dated 'Seaton Delaval Nov 1917'. Gurney had been
gassed at the third Battle of Ypres and sent home. He was based at Seaton Delaval
Hall, Northumberland, while retraining as a signalman. He described it as 'a freezing,
uncomfortable Hell of a Hole', but the house is now a welcoming and intriguing place
to visit.

Anthem for Doomed Youth

What passing-bells for these who die as cattle?
      Only the monstrous anger of the guns.
      Only the stuttering rifles' rapid rattle
Can patter out their hasty orisons.
No mockeries now for them; no prayers nor bells,
      Nor any voice of mourning save the choirs, –
The shrill, demented choirs of wailing shells;
      And bugles calling for them from sad shires.

What candles may be held to speed them all?
      Not in the hands of boys, but in their eyes
Shall shine the holy glimmers of good-byes.
      The pallor of girls' brows shall be their pall;
Their flowers the tenderness of patient minds,
And each slow dusk a drawing-down of blinds.

Wilfred Owen
(1893–1918)

In Flanders Fields

In Flanders fields the poppies blow
Between the crosses, row on row,
        That mark our place; and in the sky
        The larks, still bravely singing, fly
Scarce heard amid the guns below.

We are the Dead. Short days ago
We lived, felt dawn, saw sunset glow,
        Loved and were loved, and now we lie,
                In Flanders fields.

Take up our quarrel with the foe:
To you from failing hands we throw
        The torch; be yours to hold it high.
        If ye break faith with us who die
We shall not sleep, though poppies grow
                In Flanders fields.

John McCrae
(1872–1918)

For the Fallen

With proud thanksgiving, a mother for her children,
England mourns for her dead across the sea.
Flesh of her flesh they were, spirit of her spirit,
Fallen in the cause of the free.

Solemn drums thrill; Death august and royal
Sings sorrow up into immortal spheres,
This is music in the midst of desolation
And a glory that shines upon our tears.

They went with songs to the battle, they were young,
Straight of limb, true of eye, steady and aglow.
They were staunch to the end against odds uncounted;
They fell with their faces to the foe.

They shall not grow old, as we that are left grow old:
Age shall not weary them, nor the years condemn.
At the going down of the sun and in the morning
We will remember them.

They mingle not with their laughing comrades again;
They sit no more at familiar tables of home;
They have no lot in our labour of the day-time;
They sleep beyond England's foam.

But where our desires are and our hopes profound,
Felt as a well-spring that is hidden from sight,
To the innermost heart of their own land they are known
As the stars are known to the Night;

As the stars that shall be bright when we are dust
Moving in marches upon the heavenly plain,
As the stars that are starry in the time of our darkness,
To the end, to the end, they remain.

Laurence Binyon
(1869–1943)

Lawrence Binyon wrote this poem in September 1914 while sitting by the cliffs between
Pentire Point and the Rumps, North Cornwall. The National Trust now owns this land
and in 2001 a stone plaque was erected to commemorate the fact and bears the inscription:

For the Fallen

Composed on these cliffs 1914

The plaque also bears the fourth stanza of the poem.

High Flight (An Airman's Ecstasy)

Oh, I have slipped the surly bonds of earth
And danced the skies on laughter-silvered wings;
Sunward I've climbed and joined the tumbling mirth
Of sun-split clouds – and done a hundred things
You have not dreamed of; wheeled and soared and swung
High in the sun-lit silence. Hovering there
I've chased the shouting wind along, and flung
My eager craft through footless halls of air;
Up, up the long delirious, burning blue
I've topped the wind-swept heights with easy grace,
Where never lark nor even eagle flew;
And while, with silent lifting mind I've trod
The high untrespassed sanctity of space,
Put out my hand, and touched the face of God.

John Gillespie Magee
(1922–1941)

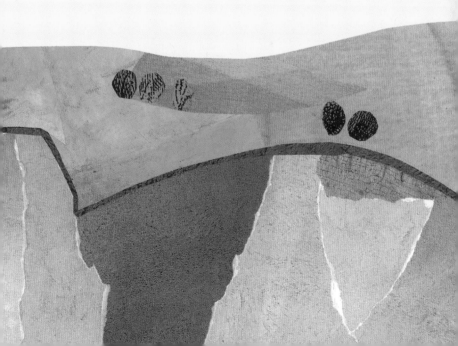

Old Favourites

'Green and Pleasant Land'

If I Could Tell You

Time will say nothing but I told you so,
Time only knows the price we have to pay;
If I could tell you I would let you know.

If we should weep when clowns put on their show,
If we should stumble when musicians play,
Time will say nothing but I told you so.

There are no fortunes to be told, although,
Because I love you more than I can say,
If I could tell you I would let you know.

The winds must come from somewhere when they blow,
There must be reasons why the leaves decay;
Time will say nothing but I told you so.

Perhaps the roses really want to grow,
The vision seriously intends to stay;
If I could tell you I would let you know.

Suppose the lions all get up and go,
And all the brooks and soldiers run away;
Will Time say nothing but I told you so?
If I could tell you I would let you know.

W. H. Auden
(1907–1973)

Jerusalem
from: *Milton*

And did those feet in ancient time
Walk upon Englands mountains green:
And was the holy Lamb of God,
On Englands pleasant pastures seen!

And did the Countenance Divine,
Shine forth upon our clouded hills?
And was Jerusalem builded here,
Among these dark Satanic Mills?

Bring me my Bow of burning gold:
Bring me my Arrows of desire:
Bring me my Spear: O clouds unfold!
Bring me my Chariot of fire!

I will not cease from Mental Fight,
Nor shall my Sword sleep in my hand:
Till we have built Jerusalem,
In Englands green and pleasant Land.

William Blake
(1757–1827)

If —

If you can keep your head when all about you
      Are losing theirs and blaming it on you,
If you can trust yourself when all men doubt you,
      But make allowance for their doubting too;
If you can wait and not be tired of waiting,
      Or being lied about, don't deal in lies,
Or being hated, don't give way to hating,
      And yet don't look too good, nor talk too wise:

If you can dream – and not make dreams your master;
      If you can think – and not make thoughts your aim;
 If you can meet with Triumph and Disaster
      And treat those two imposters just the same;
If you can bear to hear the truth you've spoken
      Twisted by knaves to make a trap for fools,
Or watch the things you gave your life to, broken,
      And stoop and build 'em up with worn-out tools:

If you can make a heap of all your winnings
      And risk it on one turn of pitch-and-toss,
And lose, and start again at your beginnings
      And never breathe a word about your loss;
If you can force your heart and nerve and sinew
      To serve your turn long after they are gone,
And so hold on when there is nothing in you
      Except the Will which says to them: 'Hold on!'

If you can talk with crowds and keep your virtue,
      Or walk with Kings – nor lose the common touch,
If neither foes nor loving friends can hurt you,

If all men count with you, but none too much;
If you can fill the unforgiving minute
    With sixty seconds' worth of distance run,
Yours is the Earth and everything that's in it,
    And – which is more – you'll be a Man, my son!

Rudyard Kipling
(1865–1936)

The Frost performs its secret ministry,
Unhelped by any wind. The owlet's cry
Came loud — and hark, again! loud as before.
The inmates of my cottage, all at rest,
Have left me to that solitude, which suits
Abstruser musings: save that at my side
My cradled infant slumbers peacefully.
'Tis calm indeed! so calm, that it disturbs
And vexes meditation with its strange
And extreme stillness. Sea, hill, and wood,
This populous village! Sea, and hill, and wood,
With all the numberless goings-on of life,
Inaudible as dreams! the thin blue flame
Lies on my low-burnt fire, and quivers not;
Only that film, which fluttered on the grate,
Still flutters there, the sole unquiet thing.
Methinks, its motion in this hush of nature
Gives it dim sympathies with me who live,
Making it a companionable form,
Whose puny flaps and freaks the idling Spirit
By its own moods interprets, every where
Echo or mirror seeking of itself,
And makes a toy of Thought.

                        But O! how oft,
How oft, at school, with most believing mind,
Presageful, have I gazed upon the bars,
To watch that fluttering *stranger*! and as oft
With unclosed lids, already had I dreamt
 Of my sweet birth-place, and the old church-tower,
Whose bells, the poor man's only music, rang
From morn to evening, all the hot Fair-day,
So sweetly, that they stirred and haunted me
With a wild pleasure, falling on mine ear
Most like articulate sounds of things to come!

So gazed I, till the soothing things, I dreamt,
Lulled me to sleep, and sleep prolonged my dreams!
And so I brooded all the following morn,
Awed by the stern preceptor's face, mine eye
Fixed with mock study on my swimming book:
Save if the door half opened, and I snatched
A hasty glance, and still my heart leaped up,
For still I hoped to see the *stranger's* face,
Townsman, or aunt, or sister more beloved,
My play-mate when we both were clothed alike!

       Dear Babe, that sleepest cradled by my side,
Whose gentle breathings, heard in this deep calm,
Fill up the interspersèd vacancies
And momentary pauses of the thought!
My babe so beautiful! it thrills my heart
With tender gladness, thus to look at thee,
And think that thou shalt learn far other lore,
And in far other scenes! For I was reared
In the great city, pent 'mid cloisters dim,
And saw nought lovely but the sky and stars.
But *thou*, my babe! shalt wander like a breeze
By lakes and sandy shores, beneath the crags
Of ancient mountain, and beneath the clouds,
Which image in their bulk both lake and shores
And mountain crags: so shalt thou see and hear
The lovely shapes and sounds intelligible
Of that eternal language, which thy God
Utters, who from eternity doth teach
Himself in all, and all things in himself.
Great universal Teacher! he shall mould
Thy spirit, and by giving make it ask.

Therefore all seasons shall be sweet to thee,
Whether the summer clothe the general earth
With greenness, or the redbreast sit and sing
Betwixt the tufts of snow on the bare branch
Of mossy apple-tree, while the nigh thatch
Smokes in the sun-thaw; whether the eave-drops fall
Heard only in the trances of the blast,
Or if the secret ministry of frost
Shall hang them up in silent icicles,
Quietly shining to the quiet Moon.

Samuel Taylor Coleridge
(1772–1834)

The fireplace in the second parlour at Coleridge Cottage, Somerset, was recently revealed during renovation work. It was here that the poet sat, in 1798, with his baby son Hartley in a wicker cradle, while he wrote this poem.

Ozymandias

I met a traveller from an antique land
Who said: Two vast and trunkless legs of stone
Stand in the desert . . . Near them, on the sand,
Half sunk, a shattered visage lies, whose frown,
And wrinkled lip, and sneer of cold command,
Tell that its sculptor well those passions read
Which yet survive, stamped on these lifeless things,
The hand that mocked them, and the heart that fed:
And on the pedestal these words appear:
'My name is Ozymandias, king of kings:
Look on my words, ye Mighty, and despair!'

Nothing beside remains. Round the decay
Of that colossal wreck, boundless and bare
The lone and level sands stretched far away.

Percy Bysshe Shelley
(1792–1822)

Sonnet

When I consider how my light is spent
      E're half my days, in this dark world and wide,
      And that one Talent which is death to hide
      Lodg'd with me useless, though my Soul more bent
To serve therewith my Maker, and present
      My true account, lest he returning chide,
      Doth God exact day-labour, light deny'd?
      I fondly ask: But patience to prevent
That murmur, soon replies, God doth not need
      Either man's work, or his own gifts; who best
      Bear his milde yoake, they serve him best, his State
Is Kingly. Thousands at his bidding speed
      And post o'er Land and Ocean without rest:
      They also serve who only stand and waite.

John Milton
(1608–1674)

If I Can Stop One Heart from Breaking

If I can stop one Heart from breaking
I shall not live in vain
If I can ease one Life the Aching
Or cool one Pain

Or help one fainting Robin
Unto his Nest again
I shall not live in Vain.

Emily Dickinson
(1830–1886)

Inversnaid

This darksome burn, horseback brown,
His rollrock highroad roaring down,
In coop and in comb the fleece of his foam
Flutes and low to the lake falls home.

A windpuff-bonnet of fáwn-fróth
Turns and twindles over the broth
Of a pool so pitchblack, féll-frówning,
It rounds and rounds Despair to drowning.

Degged with dew, dappled with dew
And the groins of the braes that the brook treads through,

Wiry heathpacks, flitches of fern,
And the beadbonny ash that sits over the burn.

What would the world be, once bereft
Of wet and of wildness? Let them be left,
O let them be left, wildness and wet;
Long live the weeds and the wilderness yet.

Gerard Manley Hopkins
(1844–1889)

Abou Ben Adhem

Abou Ben Adhem (may his tribe increase!)
Awoke one night from a deep dream of peace,
And saw, within the moonlight in his room,
Making it rich, and like a lily in bloom,
An angel writing in a book of gold: –
Exceeding peace had made Ben Adhem bold,
And to the presence in the room he said,
'What writest thou?' – The vision rais'd its head,
And with a look made of all sweet accord,
Answer'd, 'The names of those who love the Lord.'
'And is mine one?' said Abou. 'Nay, not so,'
Replied the angel. Abou spoke more low,
But cheerily still; and said, 'I pray thee then,
Write me as one who loves his fellow-men.'

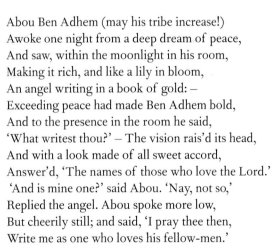

The angel wrote and vanish'd. The next night
It came again with a great wakening light,
And show'd the names whom love of God had bless'd,
And lo! Ben Adhem's name led all the rest.

Leigh Hunt
(1784–1859)

A Garden by the Sea

I know a little garden-close,
Set thick with lily and red rose,
Where I would wander if I might,
From dewy morn to dewy night,
And have one with me wandering.

And though within it no birds sing,
And though no pillared house is there,
And though the apple-boughs are bare
Of fruit and blossom, would to God
Her feet upon the green grass trod,
And I beheld them as before.

There comes a murmur from the shore,
And in the close two fair streams are,
Drawn from the purple hills afar,
Drawn down unto the restless sea:
Dark hills whose heath-bloom feeds no bee,
Dark shore no ship has ever seen,
Tormented by the billows green
Whose murmur comes unceasingly
Unto the place for which I cry.

For which I cry both day and night,
For which I let slip all delight,
Whereby I grow both deaf and blind,
Careless to win, unskilled to find,
And quick to lose what all men seek.

Yet tottering as I am and weak,
Still have I left a little breath
To seek within the jaws of death
An entrance to that happy place,
To seek the unforgotten face,
Once seen, once kissed, once reft from me
Anigh the murmuring of the sea.

William Morris
(1834–1896)

This poem does not accurately describe the garden at Red House in Bexleyheath, but William Morris used his gardens as inspiration for both his designs and his writings. He believed that they should form an integral part of the house while also being a little mysterious.

Ode on a Grecian Urn

I

Thou still unravish'd bride of quietness,
      Thou foster-child of silence and slow time,
Sylvan historian, who canst thus express
      A flowery tale more sweetly than our rhyme:
What leaf-fring'd legend haunts about thy shape
      Of deities or mortals, or of both,
          In Tempe or the dales of Arcady?
      What men or gods are these? What maidens loth?
What mad pursuit? What struggle to escape?
          What pipes and timbrels? What wild ecstasy?

II

Heard melodies are sweet, but those unheard
      Are sweeter; therefore, ye soft pipes, play on;
Not to the sensual ear, but, more endear'd,
      Pipe to the spirit ditties of no tone:
Fair youth, beneath the trees, thou canst not leave
      Thy song, nor ever can those trees be bare;
          Bold Lover, never, never canst thou kiss,
Though winning near the goal – yet, do not grieve;
      She cannot fade, though thou hast not thy bliss,
          For ever wilt thou love, and she be fair!

III

Ah, happy, happy boughs! that cannot shed
      Your leaves, nor ever bid the Spring adieu;
And, happy melodist, unwearied,
      For ever piping songs for ever new;
More happy love! more happy, happy love!
      For ever warm and still to be enjoy'd,
          For ever panting, and for ever young;
All breathing human passion far above,
      That leaves a heart high-sorrowful and cloy'd,
          A burning forehead, and a parching tongue.

Who are these coming to the sacrifice?
    To what green altar, O mysterious priest,
Lead'st thou that heifer lowing at the skies,
    And all her silken flanks with garlands drest?
What little town by river or sea shore,
    Or mountain-built with peaceful citadel,
      Is emptied of this folk, this pious morn?
And, little town, thy streets for evermore
    Will silent be; and not a soul to tell
      Why thou art desolate, can e'er return.

V

O Attic shape! Fair attitude! with brede
    Of marble men and maidens overwrought,
With forest branches and the trodden weed;
    Thou, silent form, dost tease us out of thought
As doth eternity; Cold Pastoral!
    When old age shall this generation waste,
      Thou shalt remain, in midst of other woe
Than ours, a friend to man, to whom thou say'st
    'Beauty is truth, truth beauty,' – that is all
      Ye know on earth, and all ye need to know.

John Keats
(1795–1821)

Leisure

What is this life, if full of care,
We have no time to stand and stare.

No time to stand beneath the boughs
And stare as long as sheep or cows.

No time to see, when woods we pass,
Where squirrels hide their nuts in grass.

No time to see, in broad daylight,
Streams full of stars like skies at night.

No time to turn at Beauty's glance,
And watch her feet, how they can dance.

No time to wait till her mouth can
Enrich that smile her eyes began.

A poor life this, if full of care,
We have no time to stand and stare.

W. H. Davies
(1871–1940)

Solitude

Laugh, and the world laughs with you;
      Weep, and you weep alone.
For the sad old earth must borrow its mirth,
      But has trouble enough of its own.
Sing, and the hills will answer;
      Sigh, it is lost on the air;
The echoes bound to a joyful sound,
      But shrink from voicing care.

Rejoice, and men will seek you;
      Grieve and they turn and go.
They want full measure of all their pleasure,
      But they do not need your woe.
Be glad, and your friends are many;
      Be sad, and you lose them all.
There are none to decline your nectared wine,
      But alone you must drink life's gall.

Feast, and your halls are crowded;
      Fast, and the world goes by.
Succeed and give, and it helps you live,
      But no man can help you die.
There is room in the halls of pleasure
      For a long and lordly train,
But one by one we must all file on
      Through the narrow aisles of pain.

Ella Wheeler Wilcox
(1850–1919)

The Sunlight on the Garden

The sunlight on the garden
Hardens and grows cold,
We cannot cage the minute
Within its nets of gold,
When all is told
We cannot beg for pardon.

Our freedom as free lances
Advances towards its end;
The earth compels, upon it
Sonnets and birds descend;
And soon, my friend,
We shall have no time for dances.

The sky was good for flying
Defying the church bells
And every evil iron
Siren and what it tells:
The earth compels,
We are dying, Egypt, dying

And not expecting pardon,
Hardened in heart anew,
But glad to have sat under
Thunder and rain with you,
And grateful too
For sunlight on the garden.

Louis MacNeice
(1907–1963)

The Lady of Shalott
Part I

On either side the river lie
Long fields of barley and of rye,
That clothe the wold and meet the sky;
And thro' the field the road runs by
      To many-tower'd Camelot;
And up and down the people go,
Gazing where the lilies blow
Round an island there below,
      The island of Shalott.

Willows whiten, aspens quiver,
Little breezes dusk and shiver
Thro' the wave that runs for ever
By the island in the river
       Flowing down to Camelot.
Four gray walls and four gray towers,
Overlook a space of flowers,
And the silent isle imbowers
       The Lady of Shalott.

By the margin, willow-veil'd,
Slide the heavy barges trail'd
By slow horses; and unhail'd
The shallop flitteth silken-sail'd
       Skimming down to Camelot:
But who hath seen her wave her hand?
Or at the casement seen her stand?
Or is she known in all the land,
       The Lady of Shalott?

Only reapers, reaping early
In among the bearded barley,
Hear a song that echoes cheerly
From the river winding clearly,
       Down to tower'd Camelot:
And by the moon the reaper weary,
Piling sheaves in uplands airy,
Listening, whispers ''Tis the fairy
       Lady of Shalott.'

Alfred, Lord Tennyson
(1809–1892)

The Woods of Westermain
Verse 1

Enter these enchanted woods,
> You who dare
Nothing harms beneath the leaves
More than waves a swimmer cleaves.
Toss your heart up with the lark,
Foot at pace with mouse and worm,
> Fair you fare.
Only at the dread of dark
Quaver, and they quit their form:
Thousand eyeballs under hoods
> Have you by the hair.
Enter these enchanted woods,
> You who dare.

George Meredith
(1828–1909)

The Bright Field

I have seen the sun break through
to illuminate a small field
for a while, and gone my way
and forgotten it. But that was the pearl
of great price, the one field that had
the treasure in it. I realize now
that I must give all that I have
to possess it. Life is not hurrying

on to a receding future, nor hankering after
an imagined past. It is the turning
aside like Moses to the miracle
of the lit bush, to a brightness
that seemed as transitory as your youth
once, but is the eternity that awaits you.

R. S. Thomas
(1913–2000)

My Heart Leaps Up
Written at Town-end, Grassmere.

My heart leaps up when I behold
  A rainbow in the sky:
So it was when my life began;
So it is now I am a man;
So be it when I shall grow old,
  Or let me die!
The Child is father of the Man;
And I could wish my days to be
Bound each to each by natural piety.

William Wordsworth
(1770–1850)

Wordsworth was born in Cockermouth, Cumbria (in a cottage now known as
Wordsworth House and Garden) and lived in the Lake District for most of his life. He was
passionate about the area and, in 1810, published *A Guide through the District of the Lakes*.
Wordsworth wrote the poem at Dove Cottage in Townend, Grasmere.

I Remember, I Remember

I remember, I remember,
The house where I was born,
The little window where the sun
Came peeping in at morn;
He never came a wink too soon,
Nor brought too long a day,
But now, I often wish the night
Had borne my breath away!

I remember, I remember,
The roses, red and white,
The vi'lets, and the lily-cups,
Those flowers made of light!
The lilacs where the robin built,
And where my brother set
The laburnum on his birthday, –
The tree is living yet!

I remember, I remember,
Where I used to swing,
And thought the air must rush as fresh
To swallows on the wing;
My spirit flew in feathers then,
That is so heavy now,
And summer pools could hardly cool
The fever on my brow!

I remember, I remember,
The fir trees dark and high;
I used to think their slender tops
Were close against the sky:
It was a childish ignorance,
But now 'tis little joy
To know I'm farther off from heav'n
Than when I was a boy.

Thomas Hood
(1799–1845)

The Earthly Paradise

I. An Apology

Of Heaven or Hell I have no power to sing,
I cannot ease the burden of your fears,
Or make quick-coming death a little thing,
Or bring again the pleasure of past years,
Nor for my words shall ye forget your tears,
Or hope again for aught that I can say,
The idle singer of an empty day.

But rather, when aweary of your mirth,
From full hearts still unsatisfied ye sigh,
And, feeling kindly unto all the earth,
Grudge every minute as it passes by,
Made the more mindful that the sweet days die –
– Remember me a little then I pray,
The idle singer of an empty day.

The heavy trouble, the bewildering care
That weighs us down who live and earn our bread,
These idle verses have no power to bear;
So let me sing of names remembered,
Because they, living not, can ne'er be dead,
Or long time take their memory quite away
From us poor singers of an empty day.

Dreamer of dreams, born out of my due time,
Why should I strive to set the crooked straight?
Let it suffice me that my murmuring rhyme
Beats with light wing against the ivory gate,
Telling a tale not too importunate
To those who in the sleepy region stay,
Lulled by the singer of an empty day.

Folk say, a wizard to a northern king
At Christmas-time such wondrous things did show,
That through one window men beheld the spring,
And through another saw the summer glow,
And through a third the fruited vines a-row,
While still, unheard, but in its wonted way,
Piped the drear wind of that December day.

So with this Earthly Paradise it is,
If ye will read aright, and pardon me,
Who strive to build a shadowy isle of bliss
Midmost the beating of the steely sea,
Where tossed about all hearts of men must be;
Whose ravening monsters mighty men shall slay,
Not the poor singer of an empty day.

William Morris
(1834–1896)

Although *The Earthly Paradise* was not published until 1868–70, William Morris began it while he was living at Red House, Bexleyheath, now looked after by the National Trust. Work and family commitments meant that he was only able to live in the house for five years, but certainly, at first, these were some of the happiest of his life.

Jabberwocky

'Twas brillig, and the slithy toves
    Did gyre and gimble in the wabe:
All mimsy were the borogroves,
    And the mome raths outgrabe.

'Beware the Jabberwock, my son!
    The jaws that bite, the claws that catch!
Beware the Jubjub bird, and shun
    The frumious Bandersnatch!'

He took his vorpal sword in hand:
    Long time the manxome foe he sought –
So rested he by the Tumtum tree,
    And stood awhile in thought.

And, as in uffish thought he stood,
    The Jabberwock, with eyes of flame,
Came whiffling through the tulgey wood,
    And burbled as it came!

One, two! One, two! And through and through
    The vorpal blade went snicker-snack!
He left it dead, and with its head
    He went galumphing back.

'And hast thou slain the Jabberwock?
    Come to my arms, my beamish boy!
O frabjous day! Callooh! Callay!'
    He chortled in his joy.

'Twas brillig, and the slithy toves
     Did gyre and gimble in the wabe;
All mimsy were the borogroves,
     And the mome raths outgrabe.

Lewis Carroll
(1832–1898)

Kubla Khan

In Xanadu did Kubla Khan
A stately pleasure-dome decree:
Where Alph, the sacred river, ran
Through caverns measureless to man
       Down to a sunless sea.
So twice five miles of fertile ground
With walls and towers were girdled round:
And there were gardens bright with sinuous rills,
Where blossomed many an incense-bearing tree;
And here were forests as ancient as the hills,
Enfolding sunny spots of greenery.
But oh! that deep romantic chasm which slanted
Down the green hill athwart a cedarn cover!
A savage place! as holy and enchanted
As e'er beneath a waning moon was haunted
By woman wailing for her demon lover!
And from this chasm, with ceaseless turmoil seething,
As if this earth in fast thick pants were breathing,
A mighty fountain momently was forced:
Amid whose swift half-intermitted burst
Huge fragments vaulted like rebounding hail,
Or chaffy grain beneath the thresher's flail:
And 'mid these dancing rocks at once and ever
It flung up momently the sacred river.
Five miles meandering with a mazy motion
Through wood and dale the sacred river ran,
Then reached the caverns measureless to man,
And sank in tumult to a lifeless ocean:
And 'midst this tumult Kubla heard from far
Ancestral voices prophesying war!
       The shadow of the dome of pleasure
       Floated midway on the waves;
       Where was heard the mingled measure
       From the fountain and the caves.

It was a miracle of rare device,
A sunny pleasure-dome with caves of ice!

A damsel with a dulcimer
In a vision once I saw:
It was an Abyssinian maid,
And on her dulcimer she played,
Singing of Mount Abora.
Could I revive within me
Her symphony and song,
To such deep delight 'twould win me,
That with music loud and long,
I would build that dome in air,
That sunny dome! those caves of ice!
And all who heard would see them there,
And all should cry, Beware! Beware!
His flashing eyes, his floating hair!
Weave a circle round him thrice,
And close your eyes with holy dread,
For he on honey-dew hath fed,
And drunk the milk of Paradise.

Samuel Taylor Coleridge
(1772–1834)

In November 1797 Coleridge headed out from his home (now known as Coleridge
Cottage) in the Somerset village of Nether Stowey for Lynton. Staying the night at
a 'lonely farmhouse' near Culbone he fell into a drugged sleep due to 'two grains of
Opium, taken to check a dystenery'. The idea for 'Kubla Khan' came to him in his sleep
but he was famously prevented from completing it while it was still fresh in his mind by
the interruption of 'a person . . . from Porlock'.

La Belle Dame sans Merci; A Ballad
Verses 1–12

O what can ail thee, knight-at-arms,
    Alone and palely loitering?
The sedge has withered from the lake,
    And no birds sing.

O what can ail thee, knight-at-arms,
    So haggard and so woe-begone?
The squirrel's granary is full,
    And the harvest's done.

I see a lily on thy brow,
    With anguish moist and fever-dew,
And on thy cheeks a fading rose
    Fast withereth too.

I met a lady in the meads,
    Full beautiful – a faery's child,
Her hair was long, her foot was light,
    And her eyes were wild.

I made a garland for her head,
    And bracelets too, and fragrant zone;
She looked at me as she did love,
    And made sweet moan.

I set her on my pacing steed,
    And nothing else saw all day long,
For sidelong she would bend, and sing
    A faery's song.

She found me roots of relish sweet,
     And honey wild, and manna-dew,
And sure in language strange she said –
     'I love thee true'.

She took me to her elfin grot,
     And there she wept and sighed full sore,
And there I shut her wild wild eyes
     With kisses four.

And there she lullèd me asleep
    And there I dreamed – Ah! woe betide! –
The latest dream I ever dreamt
    On the cold hill side.

I saw pale kings and princes too,
    Pale warriors, death-pale were they all;
They cried – 'La belle Dame sans Merci
    Thee hath in thrall!'

I saw their starved lips in the gloam,
    With horrid warning gapèd wide,
And I awoke and found me here,
    On the cold hill's side.

And this is why I sojourn here
    Alone and palely loitering,
Though the sedge is withered from the lake,
    And no birds sing.

John Keats
(1795–1821)

He Wishes for the Cloths of Heaven

Had I the heavens' embroidered cloths,
Enwrought with golden and silver light,
The blue and the dim and the dark cloths
Of night and light and the half light,
I would spread the cloths under your feet;
But I, being poor, have only my dreams;
I have spread my dreams under your feet;
Tread softly because you tread on my dreams.

W. B. Yeats
(1865–1939)

Traditional Gaelic Blessing

May the road rise up to meet you.
May the wind be always at your back.
May the sun shine warm upon your face,
And rains fall soft upon your fields.
And until we meet again,
May God hold you in the palm of his hand.

Anon

Index of Poets

Index of Titles

Acknowledgements

W H Auden, 'Stop the Clocks' from *Collected Poems* (Faber, 1976) and 'If I Could Tell You' from *Collected Shorter Poems 1927–1957* (Faber, 1966). Reproduced with kind permissions of Curtis Brown USA and Random House USA.

Walter de la Mare, 'Silver' and 'The Listeners' from *Selected Poems* (Faber, 2006). Reproduced with kind permissions of the Literary Trustees of Walter de la Mare and the Society of Authors as their representative.

T. S. Eliot, 'Macavity' from *Old Possum's Book of Practical Cats* (Faber, 1982) and 'The Journey of the Magi' from *Collected Poems 1909–1935* (Faber, 1936). Reproduced with kind permission of Faber & Faber and Houghton Mifflin Harcourt Publishing Company.

Robert Frost. 'The Road Not Taken' from *Collected Poems* (Jonathan Cape, 1951). Reproduced with kind permission of Penguin Random House.

Robert Graves. 'Love Without Hope' from *Poems Selected by Himself* (Penguin, 1961). Reproduced with kind permission of Carcanet Press Limited.

Seamus Heaney. 'Glenmore Sonnets: VII' from *Field Work* (Faber, 1979). Reproduced with kind permission of Faber & Faber.

Philip Larkin. 'An Arundel Tomb' from *Collected Poems* (Faber, 2003). Reproduced with kind permission of Faber & Faber.

Louis MacNeice. 'Sunlight on the Garden' from *Oxford Twentieth Century English Verse* (OUP, 1973). Reproduced with kind permission of David Higham Associates Limited.

Leo Marks. 'The Life That I Have' from *Between Silk & Cyanide* (HarperCollins, 1998). Reproduced with kind permission of The History Press.

Edna St Vincent Millay. 'Sonnet XXX' from *Selected Poems* (Carcanet, 1992). Reproduced with kind permission of Holly Peppe, Literary Executor, Millay Society (millay.org).

John Masefield. 'Cargoes' and 'Sea-Fever' from *Collected Poems* (J. M. Heinemann, 1938). Reproduced with kind permission of the Society of Authors.

Alfred Noyes. 'The Highwayman' from *Ballad & Poems* (A. N. William Blackwood & Sons, 1929). Reproduced with kind permission of the Society of Authors.

Vita Sackville-West. 'Leopards at Knole' from *Orchard and Vineyard* (The Bodley Head, 1921) and 'The Garden' from *The Garden* (Frances Lincoln, 2004). Reproduced with kind permission of Curtis Brown Group Ltd, London on behalf of The Beneficiaries of the Estate of Vita Sackville-West.

Siegfried Sassoon. 'The General' from *Oxford Book of Twentieth Century Verse* (OUP, 1973). Reproduced with kind permission of the Barbara Levy Agency.

Stevie Smith. 'Not Waving but Drowning' from *Poetry Please* (Faber, 2013). Reproduced with kind permission of Faber & Faber and New Directions.

Dylan Thomas. 'Do not go gentle into that good night' and 'Fern Hill from *Oxford Book of Twentieth Century Verse* (OUP, 1973). Reproduced with kind permission of David Higham Associates Limited and New Directions.

R. H. Thomas. 'The Bright Field' from *R. S. T Everyman's Poetry* (J. M. Dent, 1996). Reproduced with kind permission of The Orion Publishing Group.

Vernon Watkins. 'Foal' from *Oxford Book of Twentieth Century Verse* (OUP, 1973). Reproduced with kind permission of Gwen Watkins and Richard Ramsbotham.

Pavilion Books is committed to respecting the intellectual property rights of others. We have therefore taken all reasonable efforts to ensure that the reproduction of all contents on these pages is done with the full consent of the copyright owners. If you are aware of unintentional omissions, please contact the company directly so that any necessary corrections may be made for future editions.

Editor's Acknowledgements

I combine editing poetry anthologies, writing gardening books and bookselling, and I would like to thank everyone at Hatchards for their support and tolerance.

I would also like to thank Peter Taylor, Bella Cockrell and Amy Feldman at the National Trust and, as always, my agent Teresa Chris.

Much of my research was done at the Saison Poetry Library at the Royal Festival Hall in London. It has a wonderful collection of books, brilliantly helpful staff and is a joy to work in.

Many people helped me with suggestions of poems I could include. In particular, I would like to thank Ian Prince, David and Sue Gibb and Jeremy Bourne.

This may be the first anthology of poetry to be dedicated to an estate agent and a cat. Whilst compiling it I was attempting to move house and, without Mat Goss, I would have bought the wrong house, lost heart and certainly not have been in the mood to read poetry. I cannot thank him enough. Everything would have been done more quickly, but less pleasantly, without Tabitha's help.